by

Jill Bossert

ADVERTISING

PRO-
ILLUSTRATION

A Guide to Professional
Illustration Techniques
Sponsored by the
Society of Illustrators
Photography by
Marianne Barcellona

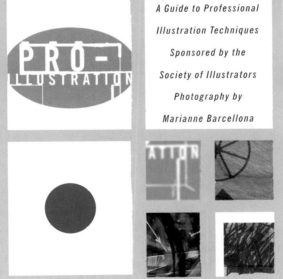

Published by
RotoVision SA
7 rue du Bugnon
1299 Crans
Switzerland

Copyright © 1997 by RotoVision
All rights reserved. Copyright under
International and Pan-American
Copyright Conventions.

No part of this book may be reproduced,
stored in a retrieval system or transmitted in any other form, or by any means,
electronic, mechanical, photocopying,
recording or otherwise, without prior
permission of the publishers.

While RotoVision makes every effort
possible to publish full and correct cred-
its for each work included in this volume, sometimes errors of omission or
commission may occur. For this
RotoVision is most regretful, but hereby
must disclaim any liability.

Distributed to the trade
in the United States:
Watson-Guptill Publications
1515 Broadway, New York, NY 10036

Distributed throughout
the rest of the world by:
RotoVision Sales Office
Sheridan House,
112/116A Western Road
Hove BN3 1DD, England
Tel. +44 1273 727268
Fax. +44 1273 727269

by Jill Bossert
Designed by Stephen Byram
Cover illustration by Stephen Byram
Design Assistant: Michael A. Cundari
Photo credit: ©1997
by Marianne Barcellona
for demonstration
photographs and portraits

Printed in Singapore
ISBN 2-88046-310-6

ASK FIRST

Images appearing in this book should not be "swiped" for any reason, including client presentation or
"comping," without the creator's permission. We appreciate your desire to use these images. Even more, we are
flattered and complimented. We encourage you to respect private intellectual property and the copyright law that
governs it. Please call before copying.   Mark Designed by the Pushpin Group, Inc.

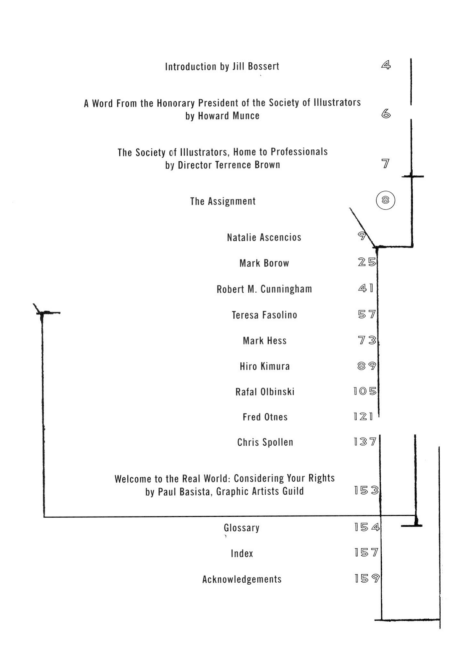

What happens when professional illustrators get an assignment? When they hang up the phone after speaking with an art director, what do they do? After they finish reading the text and specs off a fax, what next? Do they rush to their drawing boards and dash off two dozen sketches? Or do they fold up into a lotus position and chant? Where do their ideas come from? How important is research? How do ideas become graphic representations of those ideas? How many stages of approval by the client are required? What are some tricks to keep changes to a minimum? How long does the whole process take? How do they keep excited and challenged about making pictures?

The Pro-Illustration series explores these and other questions and provides answers. In each volume, nine top professionals demonstrate how they proceed from initial assignment to final illustration. In easy-to-understand steps, they'll share with you their thought processes and techniques.

By exploring a variety of methods, emerging illustrators will find the most effective way to communicate ideas. In the Pro-Illustration series many techniques will be demonstrated, so if cutting tiny pieces of frisket and wielding an airbrush—as Hiro Kimura does—is too exacting and methodical for you, perhaps breaking the rules of gravity—like Rafael Olbinski—would better suit your personality. Or consider Fred Otnes's technique and you may find that you love making complex collages.

You will discover that for an illustration to be successful, it is necessary to have a concept that is equal to the execution. Beautiful technique is not enough; the point must be made with a clear visual image that can be quickly read.

Yet, the concept can't outweigh the technique—the aim is for a nice marriage. It is a silent media—communication must be accomplished without words.

The world of illustration is as varied and inventive as each artist who inhabits it. As this series demonstrates, it's a world which asks only that you keep your eyes and minds open to possibility.

ILLUSTRATION, A FINE ART The sculptor David Smith defined commercial art as "Art that meets the minds and needs of other people," and fine art as "Art that meets the mind and needs of the artist." Illustrator and career-long educator Marshall Arisman, whose work appeared in *Pro-Illustration Volume One*, suggests that illustration can function as "one outlet for work done to meet both the artists' needs and the public's. Discoveries made in painting," he says, "can be translated into illustration by using the printed page as an entry to explore the possibility of word and image." Illustrators are artists who have chosen the printed page as their vehicle for making pictures, allowing their work to be seen by millions of people.

MEDIA IS THE MESSAGE If you look over the description of the media used by illustrators in any one of the dozens of Society of Illustrators Annuals of American Illustration, you can see an extraordinary array of possibilities open to you. Traditional methods continue to predominate: oil on canvas, watercolor and acrylic. But we see with greater frequency entries such as "Iris printouts from Illustrator 5.5 for the Macintosh computer." Artists draw using pencil, charcoal, pen and ink, pastel, crayon, and colored pencils. They make their marks on linen canvas, cotton duck, masonite, wood, vinyl, all manner of illustration board with rough or smooth finishes, and on every variety of paper from Arches watercolor blocks to Japanese rice paper. They carve or scratch out their lines in etchings, linocuts, drypoint, block prints and scratchboard. They make lithographs, monotypes, or monoprints. Those who mix their media combine any number of techniques. The collage artists and three-dimensional illustrators use any material that serves their intellectual and aesthetic needs, from centuries-old ephemera to live doves. In the Pro-Illustration series, we will show you the hows and whys of these techniques.

As in all areas of modern life, the computer is moving into illustration, and as a tool it is only as good and stimulating as the artist using it. If you are *only* interested in technique, flashy technical images will be all you'll get. If you have something to say, the computer is another medium of expression. Throughout the series we will show how the computer can be used creatively to make compelling images for reproduction.

Arisman counsels the following, which holds true for all forms of media: "Make pictures you know something about in which you have a personal interest. Consider the issue seriously and if you are sincere and honest with yourself, you will realize that you have something to say with your work beyond its *style*."

CREATIVITY Although the primary function of this book—and of the entire series—is to clearly and concisely describe the technical feats of famous illustrators, there is an aspect about making a piece of art that should be touched upon. For want of a better term, we'll call it creativity. We've tried to allude to it between the descriptions of what type of brush to use, or how to cut a perfect frisket, or what mixture of paint will produce a luminous flower petal. It cannot be taught, exactly, but it can be stimulated, and it can be allowed to, and in fact, it must be allowed to rise from within and be brought to bear upon the technical aspects of picture making. Each artist must discover it for himself or herself, and it is deeply personal and different for everyone.

As the nine artists describe the process of creating their work, invariably a moment comes when each one can no longer express that process in concrete terms. By whatever route they take to reach a satisfactory solution, and however clear the mechanics of reaching it are, there always remains a moment of mystery. Chris Spollen says, "It seems like I know what I'm doing, but sometimes it's just a gut feeling," which may, on the face of his accomplishments, appear disingenuous. Yet—there is a mysterious space that resides somewhere between the place where conscious problem-solving occurs and the technical knowledge and experience that is the execution. It is a place that no one can properly describe. It is a place where transcendent emotion, intellect, and graphic representation come together to create imagery that effectively touches others.

It is the home of creativity. And those who have been living creative lives for years know as little about it as those who have just begun to explore that mysterious territory. Time and experience does not obliterate it. Each assignment asks the artist to go there. A first-year student who creates a successful image—even under the burden of unformed skills—can share the sensation of the award-winning illustrator. By the same token, a thirty-year veteran must be able to experience the mystery, or the work will reflect a lack of spontaneity. Technique and old solutions will replace ingenuity and creativity.

The idea shared by many of the artists is this: you must allow yourself to be open to accidents. The general consensus, too, is that a certain amount of playfulness is crucial to the process. Good advice might be to indulge yourself in the things that fascinate you—the themes and meanings will take care of themselves. If you are unable to explain hard reasoning for certain choices you make, don't be alarmed—you could be right where you want to be.

Jill Bossert

A word from the honorary president of the Society of Illustrators

There's a narrow building with a red door on 63rd Street just off Lexington Avenue in New York City. Step in when you're in the neighborhood. Better yet, journey there. Come by hook or crook or by jet or jitney. Peruse the names on the bronze plaque, then try to suppress a low whistle and the word WOW!

These are the names of the artists chosen by their peers for the Society of Illustrators Hall of Fame.

Read the names again and visualize the work that has issued from those varied hands and minds. You're apt to be jolted by sheer force of the accumulative talent those names represent; and jolted still further if you ruminate on the zillions of readers who were enticed into the text of the myriad stories, books and articles, each peopled and composed into imagined places and predicaments. And think too, of the effect on the fashions and mores of their times inspired by their magazine and advertising works. In an earlier day, swipe-happy Hollywood kept a keen eye on their output and borrowed liberally from it.

In past years the Society was Home Sweet Home for many members. That's where they hung out before the migration to the suburbs. It was the social center for the profession; the Gallery, the Bar, and the Pool Table were where the members gathered after they quit their drawing boards and easels for the day.

That custom no longer obtains. Luncheon is the big gathering time now. The pool table has long since vanished to make space for the avalanche of entries for upcoming Annual Exhibitions which has become a high point of New York's graphic scene.

The building now continually hangs exhibitions on three floors. Selections from the Permanent Collection are on view in the buzzing dining room at all times. These walls reflect the unimagined visual changes that have evolved since the early days of mostly oil, wash and charcoal works. To be sure, those mediums are still widely used, but in vastly different ways as the eyes and hands behind them reflect their times. That means an exposure to the wizard's mix of today's hi-tech explosion of visual wonders.

The old days of illustrated fiction, as we nostalgically recall it, has disappeared down Memory Lane. But to replace it we have marvelous paperback book cover illustrators, jacket designers, skilled imaginers who depict the never-never land of Science Fiction, incredible renderers with surrealistic leanings, ingenious decorative artists, artists who think funny and draw funny, too, and a slew of creators who palm a plastic mouse around a magic pad to amazing effect.

The ghosts of Charles Dana Gibson, N.C. Wyeth, and Harvey Dunn, et. al., must spin in a smocked whirlwind at the sight of today's state of things. But, cool it Old Gents, your legacy still lingers. The human figure, though rendered now in endless new inventive ways, still prevails in the narrow building where you set the standards long ago.

Howard Munce
Honorary President, Society of Illustrators

HALL OF FAME LAUREATES 1958-1996

Norman Rockwell 1958	
Dean Cornwell 1959	Coby Whitmore 1978
Harold Von Schmidt 1959	Norman Price 1978
Fred Cooper 1960	Frederic Remington 1978
Floyd Davis 1961	Ben Stahl 1979
Edward Wilson 1962	Edwin Austin Abbey 1979
Walter Biggs 1963	Lorraine Fox 1979
Arthur William Brown 1964	Saul Tepper 1980
Al Parker 1965	Howard Chandler Christy 1980
Al Dorne 1966	James Montgomery Flagg 1980
Robert Fawcett 1967	Stan Galli 1981
Peter Helck 1968	Frederic R. Gruger 1981
Austin Briggs 1969	John Gannam 1981
Rube Goldberg 1970	John Clymer 1982
Stevan Dohanos 1971	Henry P. Raleigh 1982
Ray Prohaska 1972	Eric (Carl Erickson) 1982
Jon Whitcomb 1973	Mark English 1983
Tom Lovell 1974	Noel Sickles 1983
Charles Dana Gibson 1974	Franklin Booth 1983
N.C. Wyeth 1974	Neysa Moran McMein 1984
Bernie Fuchs 1975	John LaGatta 1984
Maxfield Parrish 1975	James Williamson 1984
Howard Pyle 1975	Charles Marion Russell 1985
John Falter 1976	Arthur Burdett Frost 1985
Winslow Homer 1976	Robert Weaver 1985
Harvey Dunn 1976	Rockwell Kent 1986
Robert Peak 1977	Al Hirschfeld 1986
Wallace Morgan 1977	Haddon Sundblom 1987
J.C. Leyendecker 1977	Maurice Sendak 1987
	René Bouché 1988
	Pruett Carter 1988
	Robert T. McCall 1988
	Erté 1989
	John Held Jr. 1989
	Arthur Ignatius Keller 1989
	Burt Silverman 1990
	Robert Riggs 1990
	Morton Roberts 1990
	Donald Teague 1991
	Jessie Willcox Smith 1991
	William A. Smith 1991
	Joe Bowler 1992
	Edwin A. Georgi 1992
	Dorothy Hood 1992
	Robert McGinnis 1993
	Thomas Nast 1993
	Coles Phillips 1993
	Harry Anderson 1994
	Elizabeth Shippen Green 1994
	Ben Shahn 1994
	James Avati 1995
	McClelland Barclay 1995
	Joseph Clement Coll 1995
	Frank E. Schoonover 1995
	Herb Tauss 1996
	Anton Otto Fischer 1996
	Winsor McCay 1996
	Violet Oakley 1996
	Mead Schaeffer 1996

The Society of Illustrators, home to professionals

Welcome to the Society of Illustrators, a not-for-profit educational organization founded in 1901. The mission of this Society is to promote the art of illustration. The key to the fulfillment of that mission is education. This book is a significant addition to the educational process of artists, as it is the only one created by that unique visual creator, the ILLUSTRATOR.

Art education is an ongoing process. Just look at the processes and influence displayed herein. These artists have continually sought out the works of their peers, as well as the works of the greats of the past, and added them to their own artistic stew.

Among the many venues for investigation is the Society of Illustrators. Annually, over 3,000 original works are displayed in the Society of Illustrators Museum of American Illustration in group, theme, and solo shows. The Lecture Series brings to the public the presentations of as many as ten artists in one-on-one sessions and in panel discussions. Publications of contemporary and historic illustration bring to a wide international audience the top practitioners from Hall of Famers to college-level students. Videos, slides, traveling exhibitions, and membership are other avenues that are used to spread the word.

One of the leading award-winning illustrators working today is Gary Kelley. Upon receiving a Gold Medal in the Society's Annual Exhibition, he told a story which illustrates the ongoing process of art education. Gary's studio is in Cedar Falls, Iowa, a small college town surrounded by corn fields. A job he was working on was not going well. It was time, he realized, to freshen his point of view by going "out on the road." He called an illustrator friend from Ohio. They met in Chicago to see an exhibition, on its last day, of an 18th century Spanish painter. Gary returned to Cedar Falls, fully recharged, and turned out the Gold Medal winner. That's the muse that drives the pro.

Beyond the live action of exhibitions and lectures, lies the vast study hall of the printed page. Like this publication, books on theory and creative evolution, as well as commercial and fine art reference, serve to fire one's passions when needed. Would Gary Kelley have ascended to Gold without the stimulation of that Spanish painter? Maybe, but had that exhibit in Chicago been closed, his piece might have lacked a certain, special texture.

Surely, you would enjoy having these nine artists sit down in your studio and show you how they work. Given that impracticality, their efforts will serve you as presented here. In fact, their ideas and pictures can occupy an imposing place above your board or PC. Always there to break the funk or power up weak batteries.

There is validity in the title of this series: Pro-Illustration. It is indeed a profession. An artist, whether student, novice, or pro, can benefit from the unique creative techniques of the illustrator. Because of an illustration's predetermined dimension and deadline, it must conform to scale and be on time. Created for the purpose of solving a visual need, an illustration must stay within the conceptual confines of its inducer. Palette, genre, and delivery mode (traditional or digital) may also be dictated by the client. Egads! What's left?

Ah, there's the rub. Given all of these fences, illustrators take up the challenge and find solutions that overcome the hurdles. They find the twist that communicates and also keeps them enthralled as artists. They find the edge that gives this particular job a dangerous quality. And they do it day in and day out, many of them for an entire career. With that fine-tuned mental gymnastic training, an illustrator is well suited to present both the technical and the intellectual processes of the craft.

This professionalism is not new to the industry. One of its first superstars was the pen-and-ink social satirist and cultural delineator, Charles Dana Gibson (18-67-1944). In the pages of Life, from the 1880s to the 1920s, he depicted love, liberty, and the pursuit of happiness. At a recent exhibition at the Society of over a hundred of Gibson's originals, time and again the contemporary professional illustrators wondered: "Why did he make it so difficult? Why did he add that element which must have taken a great deal of time to work out? Why did he add that extra character, architectural element, or punch line?" The answer lies in the challenge. The simple is too easy; the difficult keeps you fresh.

Look at these nine professional solutions. Easy, you say? Read the book and issue yourself the challenge.

Terrence Brown, Director
Society of Illustrators

The assignment

8" LIVE AREA

9"
LIVE AREA

Each illustrator was given the identical assignment. The initial description was simple: "A watch company is doing a conceptual campaign and your job is to illustrate the concept of "TIME."

We enclosed a spec sheet (with size specifications, which we based on a standard news magazine format) with space for an imaginary headline and advertising copy below the illustration. We then made a follow-up phone call to discuss the project more fully. For a "real" client, there would be many specifics about the company that would have to be considered, but the Pro-Illustration artists were easily able to imagine such a conceptual campaign. For the most part they were pleased for the freedom we allowed them and the wide-ranging possibilities of such an abstract idea. It should be noted here that the number of steps each artist takes to fulfill an assignment does not indicate by any measure the difficulty or ease with which they accomplish their tasks. Value is not placed on the amount of work done, but what the work produces. Some techniques are fulfilling to individuals for unknown reasons. Robert M. Cunningham will make many changes in a piece that looks utterly fresh when completed, while Mark Borow needs equipment and staff to accomplish his three-dimensional works. There is no right way. But one thing is quite clear—all these artists are perfectionists in their own way. Obsession seems to be a necessary ingredient to being a successful illustrator.

ADD ½" BLEED ALL AROUND

NATALIE ASCENCIOS LIVES
IN A WORKING-CLASS AREA OF
BROOKLYN TO SAVE ON RENT. THE
FLOOR-THROUGH APARTMENT/STUDIO
HAS FEW AMENITIES BUT A GREAT
SPIRIT OF CREATIVITY. IN THE
KITCHEN A FULL-SIZE SKELETON IN A
TUTU HANGS FROM THE CEILING
PIPES. ON THE FLOOR NEXT TO THE
OVEN ARE COOKIE SHEETS FILLED
WITH MINIATURE HANDS AND FEET
SCULPTED FOR THE MAGICAL
PUPPETS ASCENCIOS CREATES.
ALTHOUGH SHE HAS THREE ROOMS,
SHE SLEEPS IN A LOFT BED IN THE
KITCHEN WHERE HER REFERENCE
BOOKS FILL A TALL SHELF. THE REST
OF THE APARTMENT IS GIVEN UP
ENTIRELY TO PAINTING—BRUSHES ARE
SCATTERED AROUND THE FLOOR'S

perimeter, paintings in various stages of completion hang or are stacked all around. The noise of a busy city street invades. On a black-and-white checkerboard floor, Ascencios works at an easel, seated on a straight-backed chair, her dark hair gathered up, sometimes acting as a receptacle for brushes.

"I'm extremely critical of my own work," the artist says of her formal education, "No teacher was critical enough." In 1991, when she returned to New York from Paris, she studied privately with Bob Levering, who seemed to understand the lengths to which she wanted to push herself. As with most illustrators given this "Time" assignment, Ascencios was pleased with the flexi-bility we allowed. When given the opportunity to freely interpret a piece, she favors a children's storybook approach. She has discovered that when she discusses a job with a client, no matter how "loose" the assignment may seem, she tries to get an idea of where the art director is coming from. "The worst thing is when clients appear to allow complete freedom, but deep down inside, they know what they want." After determining her clients' desires as clearly as possible, Ascencios tries to stretch the concept as much as she can, either compositionally or with her use of color, "so that I can get away from what they told me they wanted. I want to be satisfied with what I do." How deeply she discusses her ideas

with clients depends on whether it's a huge campaign or a small job, how well the client knows her, and how much time she has. She will generally present two or three pencil sketches on "whatever paper fits the fax machine." She usually gives details in the sketch that will give a "nice flavor" to what's going on; she wants them to be intrigued. Because the "Time" assignment was truly left up to her, she went with the fairy tale story of Cinderella whose whole future was dependent upon the striking of the clock at midnight.

1 Ascencios works out the composition and a gestural feel of the piece in her initial pen-and-ink thumbnails.
Aware that the final work will be on a larger scale, she decides on a composition that will be satisfactory when enlarged.

2 Often she just "mindlessly sketches" until something pleases her. Here she works out some larger details and has become more satisfied with the composition. Throughout the project she changes her mind—it is a process of constant re-assessment. She will erase and go over and over areas until she is satisfied.

3 Though she's familiar with the dress of the 17th century era, Ascencios nevertheless refers to research to be certain she isn't going too far off into her own imaginary world. In this case she checked the Dover Historic Costume in Pictures.

4 She goes "overboard on the sketches" but deletes details in the finished, simpler painting. Nevertheless, she enjoys the process of drawing elements that may never make it to the finish.

5 On a white, throw-away palette Ascencios sets out the following colors: Burnt Sienna, Yellow Ochre, Burnt Umber, Viridian Green, Alizarin Crimson, Cadmium Red Light, Ultramarine Blue, Cerulean Blue, and White. She doesn't use Black, though she is "not opposed to it." Although she pre-mixes many gradations of particular colors, as she goes along she constantly throws in color changes.
She works on cotton 23- by 20-inch canvas which she stretches and gessoes herself. To create the proper proportion for the job, she tapes off a portion at the bottom.

6

7

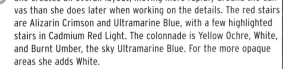

6   Ascencios begins, not by putting down a ground, but by creating an oil sketch using a Burnt Umber wash of pigment and turpentine applied with a #10 Utrecht bristle brush. This underpainting takes one day to dry.

7   With her sketches taped to the wall for reference, she blocks in areas of color to get the overall feeling of the piece. Here she uses White, Burnt Umber, and Ultramarine Blue. At this point, the piece retains the "same value idea."

8   She creates an overall layout, moving more rapidly around the canvas than she does later when working on the details. The red stairs are Alizarin Crimson and Ultramarine Blue, with a few highlighted stairs in Cadmium Red Light. The colonnade is Yellow Ochre, White, and Burnt Umber, the sky Ultramarine Blue. For the more opaque areas she adds White.

9   Using her hand, a paper towel or a little rag, she often mixes paint directly on the canvas.

10   After adding Chromium Green to her palette, she applies it to the sky. Later she has a complete change of heart and repaints the sky dark blue. When she decided to have green mice draw the carriage, she thought they would get lost in a green sky. (see Step 19) For a while the mice had been blue!
Ascencios notes that to make complete color changes this way is not very difficult and she's comfortable doing it. However, if this had been a next-day deadline she might have stuck with her original color decisions.

9

8

11

11   To put the details in the staircase, she uses a sabelette #1 round brush.

12 Ascencios usually has a "crown of brushes," which she finds "convenient." By this stage she has a very good idea of the blocking and color of the composition. Ascencios says, "a strong composition is the most important thing for keeping it all together—it's crucial. The details are a result of the composition."

13 Here Ascencios uses a mirror to check her composition. She came to this age-old technique by accident when she was in high school. Once, while carrying a drawing, she passed a mirror and noticed how it revealed the structure of the piece. Only recently she came across a reference to this practice during the Renaissance.

14 She applies Alizarin Crimson and Ultramarine Blue under the colonnade. The floor is a combination of Cerulean Blue, Yellow Ochre, and White. The Prince's coat is merely indicated at this stage using Ultramarine Blue, Alizarin Crimson, and White.

15 Using a tissue, Ascencios smears White, Yellow Ochre, and Ultramarine Blue for the clock face, the details of which come from her imagination.

12

13

14

15

16 She puts in the numerals of the clock face using a #1 round brush with Burnt Umber. Later Ascencios removed most of the details on the clock face because the image had become too complicated.

17 An overall look at the work at this stage.

In the oil sketch the Cinderella figure has two heads. Ascencios isn't sure if she prefers one big head (in keeping with the fairy tale, children's-book-style) or two heads to depict motion. After consideration, she decides that it might just look like a two-headed **18** figure and that an advertising client wouldn't like it.

The proportions of Cinderella's face are somewhat doll-like and very feminine, similar, but not exactly like the original sketch. Also, Cinderella's hair has been changed somewhat. In the initial sketch it had been a 19th century kind of hair style. Here we see a **18a** 17th century look more appropriate to the story.

The green sky and crimson stairs began to look too Christmasy to Ascencios, so she created a dark sky from a mixture of a little Alizarin Crimson with a lot of Ultramarine Blue. The sliver of moon is White with a little Ultramarine Blue and Alizarin Crimson.
Here the mice become green. As mentioned in Step 10, they had been blue, but Ascencios wiped the pigment off before they were photographed. When asked, "Why green mice?" **19** Ascencios answers, "Why not?"

Cinderella's dress is mostly White with some Ultramarine Blue and Yellow Ochre. Here she adds more detail to the fabric using a #10 brush with a mixture of Burnt Umber and Ultramarine Blue.
To maintain an overall balance, Ascencios moves all over the canvas throughout the entire process. At this point she considers her choices more slowly than when she was blocking in the composition.

20

17

16

18

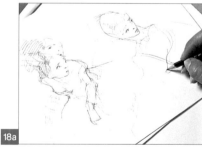
18a

20

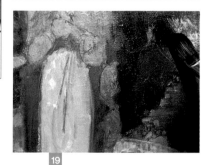
19

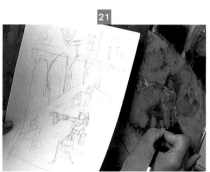

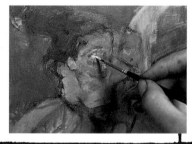

21 Referring back to her early sketches, she works on the details of the Prince's coat using Ultramarine Blue, Alizarin Crimson, and White. For all details, she refers directly to her original ideas.

22 She shapes the figure of the coachman by working on the sky, using negative space. The pumpkin carriage is Cadmium Red Light, Cadmium Yellow Light, and Yellow Ochre. The shadows on the pumpkin are Burnt Umber mixed with Viridian Green.

23 Cinderella's skin tone is Yellow Ochre, White, Burnt Sienna, a bit of Cerulean Blue, Burnt Umber, Alizarin Crimson, and Cadmium Red Light. The white of her eyes is really a grey made by mixing Burnt Umber, Ultramarine Blue, and White. Her hair is Burnt Sienna, Burnt Umber, and Viridian Green.
The skin tone on Cinderella's body is the same as her face, using less red.

24 Ascencios works with her sketches in her lap for reference.

25 The piece nearing completion.

26

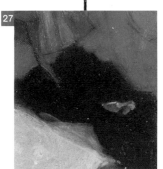

27

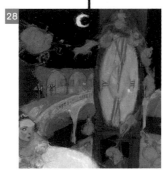

28

29

Between Step 25 and the final, Ascencios continued refining the details of the piece using the methods described above—time constraints did not allow a photographer to document each nuance.

In the final piece she has gotten rid of Cinderella's "extra" head. The floor color is more opaque, which she achieved by tinting the White with more Orange than the Burnt Umber of the underpainting.

27 To show the transparency of the glass slipper, Ascencios let the crimson of the staircase show through. The grey was made from Burnt Umber, Ultramarine Blue and White, with more White added for highlights.

28 The clock case is Burnt Umber, Yellow Ochre, Raw Sienna, and the dark area inside is Burnt Umber, and Ultramarine Blue.

29 To create more contrast between Cinderella and the background Ascencios simply adds more White to the facial colors. She changed Cinderella's hair a bit more, adding curls, accenting the 17th century style. She has also deepened the color of her ears using Alizarin Crimson, White, and Yellow Ochre.

30 Using the same colors described in Step 20, she completed the dress, adding details to the front panel and the sleeves.

The gestures of the guards and dancers are all from her tiniest thumbnail sketches. The faces of the little figures are Yellow Ochre, White, Burnt Sienna, and a little Alizarin Crimson. Their dresses are Yellow Ochre, Alizarin Crimson, Cerulean Blue, and Burnt Umber. Finally, she fills the sky with White stars.

26

31

Color, Ascencios says, helps to keep a composition together. She had considered putting different colors on all the dancers, but ultimately, she didn't want the distraction. She includes only those details necessary to keep the overall feeling of the piece intact. She waits until the paintings are dry before she messengers or FedExes her work to the client. If she has a tight deadline, she'll use Wingel, a dryer, to speed the process. She rarely, if ever, makes changes after the job is delivered.

30

31

Time Inc. 1995 Annual

top: "Grace Paley's Enormous Changes at the Last Minute"
bottom left: "Alice in Wonderland,"   bottom right: "Deep Blue vs. Kasparov"

"Evander Holyfield vs. Mike Tyson"

top: Diptych - scene from "Carmen," bottom left: Clark Gable, bottom right: Jodie Foster

top: Diptych - scene from "Carmen," bottom left: Madonna, bottom right: Woody Allen

left: Julio Bocca
right: "Untitled"

natalie
ascencios

top: Yasir Arafat, bottom: Ray Charles

N. Ascencios received her BFA from Parsons School of Design in 1993, where she was influenced by Bob Levering. She also studied in Paris for her undergraduate and graduate degrees. Included in the Society of Illustrators National Student Scholarship Competition in 1993, she has had work in the Society's Annuals of American Illustration and received a Silver Medal in 1995. She has also appeared in American Illustration 13 and 14 and received First Place in the Jim Henson Muppet Design Competition. In addition to the Society of Illustrators and The Jim Henson Gallery, her work has been exhibited at the Bergdorf Goodman Invitational Group Show for the Fifth Avenue Windows. Her clients include *Time, Rolling Stone, The New Yorker, New York, Entertainment Weekly, Esquire, Penthouse, GQ, The New York Times Book Review, Omni, Musician,* Paramount/Viacom, Simon & Schuster, St. Martin's Press, Viking Penguin, and Blue Sky Productions.

PROPART,
(ALSO KNOWN AS
MCCONNELL AND BOROW),
ONE OF NEW YORK'S TOP MODEL
MAKING OUTFITS, IS LOCATED IN
AN INDUSTRIAL BUILDING WHERE
THE DELICIOUS AROMA FROM A
NEARBY ITALIAN BAKERY WAFTS
UP THE STAIRS. MARK BOROW
RUNS THE COMPANY, THOUGH HE
CONSULTS FREQUENTLY WITH
JERRY MCCONNELL, WHO GAVE HIM
HIS START 15 YEARS AGO AND IS
STILL AN ACTIVE PARTNER. THE
SPRAWLING SPACE INCLUDES A
MACHINE SHOP, TWO ENORMOUS
WORKROOMS, A SPRAY ROOM,
KITCHEN AND AN OFFICE.
PORTIONS OF OLD JOBS ARE
EVIDENT: SOME OF THE MANY
FAMOUS ABSOLUT VODKA ADS
MCCONNELL AND BOROW
CONSTRUCTED, A HOUSE FACADE,

miniature trees, and various body parts. Borow keeps four assistants on staff but uses lots of free-lance people, depending on the project. For this job, his "major assistant" was Peter Erickson.

Upon receiving an assignment Borow tries to focus on the product being sold and how the client wants to sell it. He feels most clients have some idea of the direction in which they want to go, but our "Time" assignment gave Borow more leeway than he's accustomed to. He's found that with model making, agencies generally have a concept and even ideas of the visuals they're working towards before they even come to him.

For this assignment, Borow not only wanted to come up with a good concept, he also wanted to show off what he does well by constructing a miniature set, rather than a single product piece. It is important to remember that whatever Borow fabricates must be taken to a photographer to be shot.

He started thinking about the meaning of watches, of time itself. He talked to a lot of people about various ideas. One friend, a copywriter, threw headlines at him. Borow thinks in visuals and though he didn't use any of the headline ideas, one moved him in a particular direction. The copywriter mentioned the word "monumental." Borow thought about the Pyramids as being monumental as well as timeless. Consulting his large reference library he looked through some books on Egypt which helped clarify his idea.

Experience has taught him that a set like this has certain constraints, so he had to have a very strong visual. He knew the drama he wanted as well as the angle. He also wanted to avoid trying to simulate a vast desert, which would require an enormous set. Reference indicated that in The Valley of the Kings in Egypt, sharply angled hills behind one of the

tombs limited the horizon. This bit of reference would help him "cheat' yet remain accurate.

Borow tries to give the photographers who shoot his sets a lot of "bleed" so they can "play with the lighting." While trying to remain versatile, with 3-dimensional work "you have to nail it down in advance. You can't erase it later." However, he notes, 2-dimensional illustrators can make changes as they work, but in 3D, changes that require altering the lighting source, camera angle, or tone, take place in the photographer's studio.

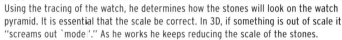

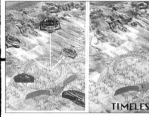

① For reference, Borow consults his books on Egypt and photographs a borrowed Rolex watch from various angles.

② He scans watch images into his computer's Photoshop program.

③ Having decided on the size and angle of the watch, Borow has printed out the image. Here he makes a tracing using a mechanical pencil with a medium soft .07 lead.

Using the tracing of the watch, he determines how the stones will look on the watch pyramid. It is essential that the scale be correct. In 3D, if something is out of scale it "screams out `model'." As he works he keeps reducing the scale of the stones.

④ He scans the finished drawing into Photoshop and combines it with a scanned-in reference picture from the Egyptian book.

⑤ On the left is one concept Borow played with: the "watch aliens" build a monument in their own image with the help of the tiny humans (made by duplicating a stick figure using the Clone Tool in Photoshop). Without the aliens' aid, the humans could not move the stones. The sketch on the right shows the watch being constructed by the ingenuity and sheer numbers of the humans.

At this point, the sketches were faxed to me. We decided on the simpler sketch for two reasons. Borow feared the alien ships were a bit "hokey," though he thought they were "funny." I felt it looked like an "invasion of the alien watches" and they were destroying rather than building the man-made structure with lasers.

Borow's second consideration was how much time he has versus how much work there is. To create the star ships and make them appear to be flying was too complicated for the time he had allotted for the project.

⑥ He begins to plan the size of everything. There is always something in a miniature set that will dictate the scale. In this case, aside from how well the set will fit into the studio, it had to do with the smallest-sized person available to Borow. He scaled everything to "Z scale figures" in the scaling system used for making model train sets. At a 1:220 proportion, Z scale is the smallest in which any detail can be discerned. From the drawing created in Step 3 he calculates how much everything else has to be blown up. The people in the drawing are 1/16 of an inch high. The Z scale people are 1/4 inch high, so everything in the drawing had to be blown up four times. Here he marks out different areas with a red pen.

⑦ He does a straight-on front view illustration of the watch in Illustrator 6.0 program which he then enlarges to full size: 24 inches.

8 He uses the printed-out 24-inch watch face as a template. He and his staff construct a mock-up by putting two pieces of 4-foot by 8-foot plywood together and placing urethane foam and foamcore to indicate the height and placement of the mountains. Borow looks at the rough set through a camera lens and makes adjustments.

9 To construct the watch "pyramid" Borow spray-glues the watch drawing on 4 lb. urethane foam, a "great carving foam." Though working with the material is a little dusty, it has a stone-like texture. The rough shapes are cut out with a band saw, though this could be done by hand.

10 Here the left and right sides and the watch face have been roughly cut out. The circle within the face has been cut out and recessed.

11 Sanding down the edges using a little stick with sandpaper spay-glued on to it. This keeps everything at right angles and sharp. If done by hand, it gets soft.

12 Using an Olfa knife, similar to an X-Acto knife, but with "a nice long blade," he cuts away some details.

13 Borow's assistant, Peter Erickson, makes the "pyramid" stairs using strips of styrene. He applies acrylic solvent (in squeeze bottle) to adhere the pieces. Because there were a number of staircases, they made one section, placed it in a vacuum form—a piece of equipment that molds plastic over a preexisting form—and duplicated it several times, though each staircase could be constructed by hand if a vacuum form is not available. Or, Borow suggests, vacuum form stairs are available in a variety of sizes at architectural model miniature suppliers. Also, model clapboard siding in tiny scale can be substituted as stairs.

14 The support base for the stairs is made of Gatorboard, the brand name of a foamcore-like material that's permeated with a resin to give it a hard surface. The open sides of the stairs will be covered with urethane foam.

15 He makes the knob winder using the same technique as in Step 9.

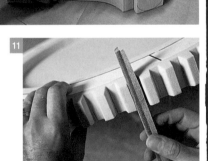

After sanding the sides of the watch he draws lines to indicate stonework using a rig made of pieces of plexiglass stacked to the proper height. He runs a #2 pencil on the side so it will always be level. Keeping the pencil sharp leaves a stone-like indentation in the soft foam.

17 The vertical lines are painstakingly done by hand.

18 Borow does the top stones using a ruler, ascribing the lines.

19 Erickson does the concentric circles on the watch face using a compass with an extender.

20 Constantly referring to the sketch, the free-standing watch is constructed by putting the sections together with a glue gun.

All the elements of the set (watch, stairs, people, mountains) will go on 4-foot by 8-foot plywood flats taken from old sets and bolted together. The sections have been "framed in" by 2-inch by 3-inch pine strips beneath. Cross pieces keep the panels from warping and aid in transporting the set to the photographer's studio. (The base as we see it here, has been painted white, to help in the photography of the "how to" steps. Otherwise, at this stage, it would be a "messy old board.")

21 The watch pyramid is given a sand-colored ground using off-white latex paint—which is less expensive than acrylics—mixed with a small amount of acrylic for color: Ochre, Burnt Umber, a little Black and a little White. Borow puts the paint in 2-pint cups and applies it with a foam brush, which allows him to get into the urethane foam better and leaves no brush marks.

22 Because it's important to get the "numerals" in the right spot, Borow uses another printout as a template, from which he cuts out the "numeral" holes. Carved foam circles and rectangles, which have been painted and had "stones" drawn on them, are glued down.

23 Cracks have been filled in with spackle, allowed to dry and given a light sanding before the "stone" surface is painted, which is "a big pain." Borow has mixed four variations of Greys, Ochres and Browns. He and his staff painted every single stone a different color because "in nature stones are never exactly the same color. It gives the piece more depth."
At this point, Borow decided the colors were still harsh, so Assistant Naomi Wilson went in with a watered-down version of the original Ochre color and gave the entire watch a light wash using a dry brush so everything would blend nicely. This whole process took two days.

24 Erickson builds a basic Gatorboard structure of the sloping background mountains. Then he attaches a piece of yellow, 1-inch urethane foam. He's positioning some old mountains from another job just to get started. To attach foam to foam he uses Super 90 3M Spray Glue. Here the set is basically together as a unit.
At this point, the elements are traced onto the set with a red pen to indicate the position of all the elements.

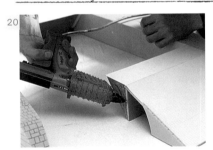

25 For the pathway leading up to the pyramid (its position marked in red), Borow bought vacuum form sheets of Styrene miniature stone pattern from the Plastruct company. He spray-glues it down.

26 After carving the mountains using Olfa knives and saws, they use a Sureform Rasp (pictured at left) to give the final texture to the mountains. Running a wire brush through the foam gives it the look of rivulets. "The foam itself is great—when you snap it, it makes beautiful craggy shapes all by itself."

27 Mixing up baking soda with Ochre, Black, White, and Burnt Umber pigments for the sand. Borow mixes the sand to match the paint color and vice versa, so they work together.
The baking soda sand is a bit lighter than the stone-colored watch which will make the watch stand out—although they will look as if they come from the same area.

28 Here he paints the whole set using a regular bristle brush because the brush strokes won't be visible.

29 A background piece of Gatorboard (see step 24) is affixed behind the mountains. It's carved out to look like sand dunes, then painted. Here the seams are being spackled.

30 Decorating the set. Using bass wood strips, Erickson has made scaffolding that goes against the "wall" of the watch pyramid. The strips are cut with an X-Acto blade and glued with Zap Gap which is similar to Krazy Glue. Areas of the pyramid are cut away to give the impression that they're still being built by the tiny figures. "You can only catch a hint of these details in the final shot," Borow says regretfully.

31 Earlier, Naomi Wilson spray-painted basic flesh tones on all the white Styrene figures, which were ordered from Walthers, a model train accessory distributor. She used Design Master Spray Paints, which are not as shiny as, and have more color variety than the more readily available Krylon brand. Here Borow is starting to paint clothing on the figures.

32 Wilson continues the job, painting the clothes in a basic dark range of blue and green acrylic paints—the colors are in keeping with what Borow imagined were the fabrics available when the pyramids were being built. Wilson painted two thousand figures separately. "She really got into it," Borow says.

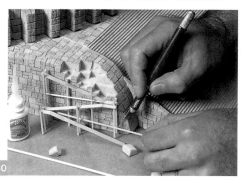

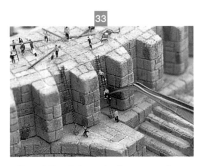

33 To save time at the photographer's, as many figures as possible were glued onto the surface of the set before it was transported. They were affixed with a dab of rubber cement so they could be moved if necessary. Using tweezers Erickson places the men climbing up ladders, making "little narratives."

34 The "little people" are carrying the internal works of the clock up the stairs. Borow insists that these kinds of details gives the overall piece a sense of authenticity. The watch hands, which can only be seen in the final shot, are bass wood colored with a Magic Marker. Bass wood is hard enough to hold its shape in such tiny proportions, but soft enough to carve.

35 Borow and his staff have packed up the set, which they took apart where the two 4-foot by 8-foot boards were bolted together. They constructed a foamcore box in which to transport the watch and all the people. Wrapping everything in bubble wrap, they traveled by van to photographer Steve Bronstein's studio.
The white tape hides the seam (where the set was disassembled for transporting). Erickson will paint it the same color as the sand.

36 The background piece is placed behind the set.

37 Using a fine strainer, the whole set is dusted with a layer of baking soda sand. Because it's non-toxic, no respirators are needed.

38 With acrylic paints and a sponge, Erickson touches up the mountains.

39 Photographer Steve Bronstein begins to determine the best lighting arrangement.

40 Erickson lays clay down in a seam (they always carry clay around to fill any holes and pockets that might be visible through the camera).

41 They sift sand everywhere on the set except on the watch pyramid itself.

42 Brushes leave marks so they shape the sand using "air in a can," an aerosol air spray.

43 Because the sand was "too perfect," Borow used a stick to add texture on the path where people would be walking. Here he takes a brush to "rough it up a little."

44 To create more irregularities, he shakes more sand over the set.

45 Borow and Bronstein confer, looking at the layout as well as enlarged Polaroids that have been taken throughout the lighting process.
Borow discusses the drama of the piece. To accomplish more drama, Bronstein changes the angle a bit. As a result, the set is not quite large enough on the right side and corrections must be made digitally in the final (see Step 47).

46 To help with the atmosphere Bronstein shines his lights through plexiglass. He has used diffusion to soften the background and warm gels to warm the overall color. He tested different films—one made the sand look like snow. The one they used was more accurate and very rich. The final was shot on 2 1/4 film with a very wide-angle lens for drama.

For the final illustration Borow scans Bronstein's photograph into the computer and digitally extends the mountains in the upper right side to compensate for the angle change in Step 45.
Borow has worked with Bronstein for over ten years. Similar in age and background, they "have an understanding and communicate well." Though this is not the case with all photographers, in general, Borow says he can interpret what people want.
After the jobs are completed most sets and props are thrown away. In this case, Borow saved the watch and the little people.

45

NBA Jam Lava Ball, Acclaim, basketball: actual size

top: SAP University, SAP America, Inc., 16 x 16 inches, bottom left: Sony Collapsed House, Sony, Scale: 1/2 inch = 12 inches, bottom right: TNT Eiffel Tower, TNT Mailfast, 5 feet high

A DISASTER IS ABOUT TO HAPPEN.

The smoke has cleared. The rubble settled. Adjusters have come and gone.

Then it happens.

Nothing.

No property compensation. No business interruption payments. No rebuilding.

The fate of an entire company depends on an insurance check that, because of slow claims handling or a shortage of cash, may be delayed. And delayed.

Until it's too late.

At INA Special Risk Facilities, Inc., a CIGNA company, we stay in business by making sure our customers do.

So we'll pay an insured loss like this promptly—even if our reinsurer doesn't. Then if someone waits, it's us.

We can open an on-the-spot claims office. And staff it with specialists from around the country, to assess property and business interruption losses, and issue third party checks as soon as possible.

We even sell salvage. And warehouse undamaged goods.

Why do we do all this?

Because at CIGNA we know that most businesses can survive anything—except the wrong insurance.

INA Special Risk Facilities, Inc.
a CIGNA company

*INA Special Risk Facilities, Inc. is the marketing company for products underwritten by the Insurance Company of North America.

Cigna Exploded Factory, Cigna Insurance Co., building: 24 x 30 inches

top: Ant, Capital Vectors, 8 inches long
bottom: Harmon Music Car, Harmon, 5 feet long

top: Supermarket, *ActMedia*, 5 feet wide x 16 feet long
bottom left: Gameboy Yard, Nintendo, 5 x 10 feet,   bottom right: Loch Ness Monster, AT&T, monster: 20 inches tall, set: 8 feet across

Ford Ranger Neighborhood, Ford, 16 x 16 feet

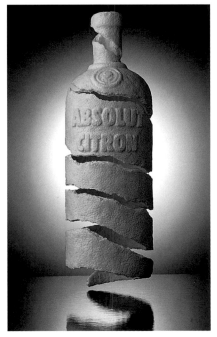

top left: Absolute L.A., Absolut Vodka/Seagram's, swimming pool: 5 feet long
top right: Absolute Appeal, Absolute Vodka/Seagram's, bottle 14 inches tall
bottom left: Absolute Miami, Absolut Vodka/Seagram's, bottle building: 18 inches tall
bottom right: Absolute Nantucket, Absolut Vodka/Seagram's, bottle dock: 8 feet tall

Mosaics, American Express, 20 x 20 inches

Mark Borow attended the Rhode Island School of Design, where he earned a Bachelor of Fine Arts degree in 1978. Borow worked free-lance as an editorial illustrator for book and magazine publishers, and as a three-dimensional illustrator he created window displays for Cartier and Tiffany & Co. Between his free-lance projects, he worked as Jerry McConnell's part-time studio assistant and quickly learned all aspects of the business. McConnell & Borow officially became partners, incorporating in 1983.

Under Borow's guidance, the company has completed many award-winning projects for a long list of clients including the advertising agencies Ammirati Puris Lintas, Grey, J. Walter Thompson, Kirshenbaum & Bond, Leo Burnett, McCann Erickson, Ogilvy & Mather, Saatchi, TBWA/Chiat Day, and Young & Rubicam. Among his recently completed and ongoing projects are Absolut, Acclaim (NBA Jam), American Express, AT&T, Bacardi, Budweiser (Bud Bowl I & II), IBM, Kodak, Miller Lite, RCA, TNT Mailfast, and USSB.

A WOODED ROAD IN THE BACK COUNTRY OF CONNECTICUT LEADS TO ROBERT CUNNINGHAM'S HOME. IT IS A SYLVAN SETTING, SURROUNDED BY LUSH TREES AND GARDENS, WITH A LARGE POND BEHIND THE HOUSE. AN OLD COVERED WELL STANDS BETWEEN THE HOUSE AND THE BARN WHERE HE HAS HIS STUDIO. THE LOW-CEILINGED FARMHOUSE, WITH ITS RAFTERS AND FIREPLACE, IS ENLIVENED BY MANY OF THE ARTIST'S WORKS ON THE WALLS. THE BOLD CARIBBEAN COLORS OF ONE OF HIS PAINTINGS LIGHTS UP A RUSTIC CORNER WHILE BASKETS HANG ON HEAVY BEAMS ABOVE.

In his large, light-filled studio, Cunningham keeps boxes full of his small, color roughs which he sometimes likes better than his finishes because "they have more feeling. A drawing is like a violin and piano sonata as opposed to a full orchestration." After discussing the project with me, Cunningham decided not to go after anything too literal. As he thought about "Time" a runner came to mind. Then he wanted to show the sun shining on the runner at different times of the day—the light would change on the figure and cast three or four different shadows. Unable to make it work graphically, he abandoned the idea. His next thought was to have the runner crossing the finish line of a 100-meter race but he didn't find any reference that satisfied him. However, while exploring the finish-line reference, he saw "this one fellow who looked different to me than the other athletes. I wanted the runner to represent Anyman, not a particular 22-year old in the Olympics." As the idea progressed, Cunningham felt that distance also represented "Time," to him. Because he's from Kansas, the vast horizon of wheat fields on the Plains seemed a good way to imply distance.

It is important to remember that to accommodate our time constraints for this book, Cunningham redid from scratch an illustration he had already completed, so our photographer could document the steps. He and his wife, Jean (also an artist and closely involved with her husband's work), want to stress that when he works on a real job, the progression of steps is not as "neat" as they appear here. He constantly makes changes and reworks ideas.

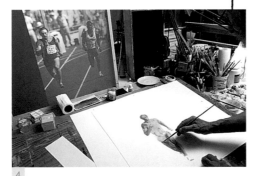

1 Cunningham makes many thumbnail pencil sketches on bond paper to help him decide what direction to take. The sketches can become quite abstract as he considers different solutions.

2 The photographic reference for the finish line idea (the center color sketch) was of blurred figures going across the line. "That's an okay image," Cunningham says, "but photography does it just as well as art, maybe better."

3 He makes full-color sketches from a number of his thumbnails to see what the color "feels like." He saves his palette so he can refer to it later (see Step 10).

4 Cunningham works standing up at a drawing board lit by a fluorescent lamp. The reference he finally decides upon is from Focus on Sports, a sports stock library he's used for years. With a rear projection system the reference slide is projected onto a screen right above his drawing board. He has a remote control to turn the projector on and off as he works. With rear projection he needn't be in the dark in order to refer to his reference. He's been using this system for 30 years and for him "it's almost like being there. Everything's frozen in time."

5 For his illustrations, Cunningham does not like to work up more than 50%. "It becomes something different when it's too big." A good size is 18- by 24-inches, and sometimes even smaller, though he's worked as large as 3- by 4-feet. For larger pieces, he paints at an easel and must rearrange the projector and screen.
Working on a Strathmore Bristol 3-ply board, he lays down the silhouette shape of the figure using Liquitex Raw Sienna. He uses Liquitex paints exclusively. Raw Sienna is the "local color that works with anything" as a medium tone. It is the ground for the basic flesh of his figures. He paints everything with bristle brushes except when he's working very small—then he uses Winsor & Newton Series 7 red sable brushes.

6 He puts the shadows on the figure by mixing Raw Umber and Raw Sienna. For warm tones he uses Reds, while Blues and Greens make "coolish" tones.

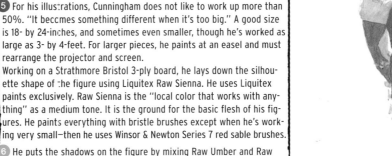

7 The square shape behind the running figure is Mars Black. Ivory Black is "too cool." The red highlight around the runner's head is Cadmium Red Light.

As he works, Cunningham shifts two old, "L"-shaped mattes like a frame around the picture plane to help decide on the cropping of the pictures. He doesn't refer to the thumbnails—which were just tools in the early, decision-making process. Once he begins the painting proper, he's "winging it," because "the colors change everything. It's a kind of evolution."

8 On a bond paper palette he mixes the undertone colors for the wheat fields on either side of the road. The colors are: Cadmium Orange, Cadmium Yellow Light, Hooker's Green, and Black.

9 He applies the underpainting to the wheat landscape. Although it's not evident in the photograph, Cunningham has changed the position of the horizon line. "It's a gut thing, not a head thing." When he's done something that he doesn't like, he just paints it out with gesso.

10 Because he likes the color of the track in one of his full-color sketches, he copies it using Red Oxide, Cadmium Red Light, Yellow Oxide, and a very small amount of White. When he applies the paint, he says it's better if the paper shows through to keep it looking fresh.

11 The highway color is Raw Umber, Ultramarine Blue, Black and White, "a fairly opaque color."

12 The large, darker cloud bank in the upper right is created by mixing Raw Umber, Ultramarine Blue, Black and White. Cunningham pushes the warm by using more Raw Umber than Blue. The slightly lighter clouds are the reverse, made by pushing the Ultramarine over the Raw Umber. For the whitish clouds, he uses the same colors as above, but with a lot of water, making a kind of glaze.

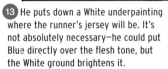

13 He puts down a White underpainting where the runner's jersey will be. It's not absolutely necessary—he could put Blue directly over the flesh tone, but the White ground brightens it.

14 He checks the image in a big mirror he always keeps behind him while he paints. "Things show up that you didn't notice."

15 The work up to this point.

The jersey is Ultramarine Blue with White. After deciding to put a red circle in the center of the jersey, he applies White over the Blue so the Red will be bright and clean. He uses Cadmium Red Light, which, he says, often appears darker when reproduced.

Cunningham points out that he's made many changes to arrive at this stage. For example, the jersey had been painted red at one point; also, the runner's shoulders had been much bigger so he carved them down to correct the proportion.

17 The shorts are Raw Umber mixed with White. The shadows are painted with a sable brush. Here he puts a Black accent on the shorts.

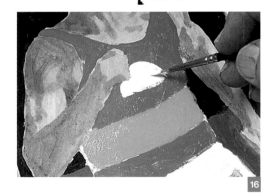

Cunningham feels it's better to have a combination of opacity and transparency. On top of the opaque road color (see Step 11) he applies the same colors (Raw Umber, Ultramarine Blue, Black and White) more transparently and adds just a touch of Dioxazine Purple, though he cautions that if the reproduction of this piece is too purple, it can be "sickening."

19 Using his thumb, he rubs the color to get it even and to give the effect of a good wash. If he's laid down too much paint, he spreads it with his whole hand.

20 To vary the flatness on the wheat field, he applies an over-painting using Yellow Oxide and White.

21 He gets dimension at the edge of the wheat field using Raw Umber, White and Black. He may have accidentally gotten a touch of Ultramarine Blue on the brush, "but it works just fine."

To create the runner's shadow he first put down Black over the roadway and then decided it needed to be lightened a bit. Using a bristle brush he scumbles over it with a Grey, made simply with Black and White.

Cunningham decides on the shapes of the three black shadows after making one of them. "Once you make one thing, it's easy to relate it to another. It's extremely important to cover the paper as soon as possible so things can relate to each other."

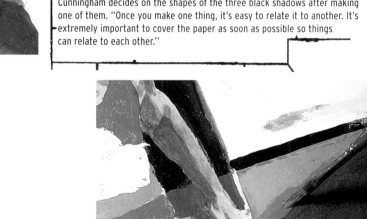

23 He draws two pencil lines with a ruler to make the border around the piece and covers the pencil marks with Raw Sienna and White.

24 The red stripe on the shorts is a mix of Cadmium Red Light with White.

25 The doors are Cadmium Red and White. "The doors are repeated symbols of the rectangle the runner is currently in. They represent different times."

26 He puts the shadows in the jersey using Ultramarine Blue, White, and Black. Cunningham had the most trouble with the runner's face. "If you don't have subtle definition in the features, it can look flat and strange."

27 The flesh on the runner's leg is Cadmium Red Light, Yellow Oxide, and White. He adds more White at the top of the thigh.

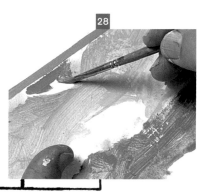

28 The bright sky color is Ultramarine Blue and White.

29 The divider line in the road is white over the black roadway. Where the runner's shadow is, Cunningham first puts Black over the line so the shadow won't be too bright. Then he applies Ultramarine with a touch of Dioxazine Purple over the Black.

30 The flesh in the face is Cadmium Red Light, Yellow Oxide, and White.

He adds White to highlight the flesh color of the nose. **31**

Cunningham has some advice: "Have fun. But discipline is crucial, you've got to produce. Not only is your career on the line, so is the art director's who hired you." Throughout his career Cunningham has been given a lot of freedom. "So," he says, "when a piece is bad it's usually my fault." He doesn't generally do preliminary sketches, though there have been times when he's had to show one. Sometimes, if there's a technical problem he'll do a pencil sketch. But he doesn't want to use up his juices; he'd rather completely redo the piece than overwork it.

His deadlines determine how long he works on a piece: if he's got four weeks, he'll take four weeks. "Sometimes I'm lucky and I hit what I want right away. Sometimes I never get it." And sometimes he ends up using what he started with in the first sketch, but he has to "go through the woods" before he comes out where he started.

He spends as much time on a spot illustration as he does for a poster. He just "does the work."

When the job is complete, he'll wrap it up and leave it on the covered well to be picked up by FedEx.

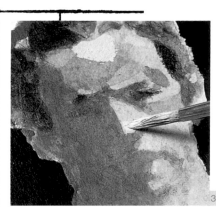

top: "Dutchess County," acrylic on panel
bottom: "Porch," acrylic on paper, H.J. Heinz, Bennett Robinson, Art Director

"Spring Training," acrylic on paper, *Lithopinion*, Robert Hallock, Art Director

"Eleuthera Express," acrylic on paper, *Lustrare*, Don Martiny, Art Director

"Sprinter," acrylic on paper, U.S. Postal Service, Dave Foote, Art Director

robert m.
cunningham

top: "Grouper Fishermen," graphite and acrylic on paper, *Lustrare*, Don Martiny, Art Director
middle: "Landing at Twin Coves," acrylic on canvas, *Lustrare*, Don Martiny, Art Director
bottom: "Red Fin Fish, Argentina," acrylic on paper, *Sports Illustrated*, Harvey Grut, Art Director

"Folly," acrylic on paper, *Lustrare*, Don Martiny, Art Director

"Kent Reservoir," acrylic on paper, "Art for Survival," United Nations Environmental Programme, Charlotte Braids, Art Director

55

robert m.
cunningham

Robert M. Cunningham was born in Kansas and attended the University of Kansas, Kansas City Art Institute, and the Art Students League in New York where he worked with Kuniyoshi, Bosa and Corbino. His illustrations have appeared in America's leading periodicals, and his corporate clients include DuPont, General Electric, Mobil, Alfa Romeo, AT&T, IBM, American Express, Exxon, New York Racing Association, Metropolitan Opera, New York Philharmonic, NYNEX, Alcoa, and others including airlines, banks, and broadcasting companies. He was the sole designer of the 1980 Summer and Winter Olympic Stamps for the U.S. Postal Service. His work has been exhibited at the Smithsonian Institution, The New-York Historical Society, in several group shows as well as a one-man show in New York, and in the major graphics organizations including the Society of Illustrators, where he has received Gold and Silver Medals as well as their Hamilton King Award.

top: "Cadaver 1," charcoal, bottom: "Cadaver 2," charcoal

F

TERESA FASOLINO'S
TWO RABBITS RUN
AROUND HER MANHATTAN
APARTMENT IN CIRCLES,
THEIR NAILS CLICKING ON
THE HARDWOOD FLOOR.
BELOVED PETS, THEY
ALSO ACT AS MODELS
FOR THE ARTIST.
HER STUDIO HAS
PORTRAITS OF BUNNIES
ON THE WALLS,
STRAW ON THE FLOOR
WHERE THE RABBITS EAT,
AND A LITTER BOX, AS
WELL AS MANY

*reference files and books.
Paint and old brushes
surround a beautiful, impres-
sionistic drawing board—it's
where Fasolino wipes off excess
paint. The TV is for watching
C-SPAN while she works.
The first thing Fasolino does
when approached by a client is
to ask what the piece will be used
for. Do they have an idea, and if
so, do they have a sketch or layout? When a client gives her carte
blanche to come up with the concept it's very exciting, though generally, she is presented with "an
idea that's already been approved."
She tries to envision something
that will really please the client,
not something that merely solves
the problem. If possible, she'll use
the job to showcase her rabbits.
For this job, her first thought was
"rabbit with a watch," but she wor-
ried that the rabbit's wrist would
be too thin, so she considered a
rabbit with a pocket watch. Or
maybe a rabbit with an hourglass.
Having considered all three types
of time pieces, she decided to use
them all to solidify the theme.*

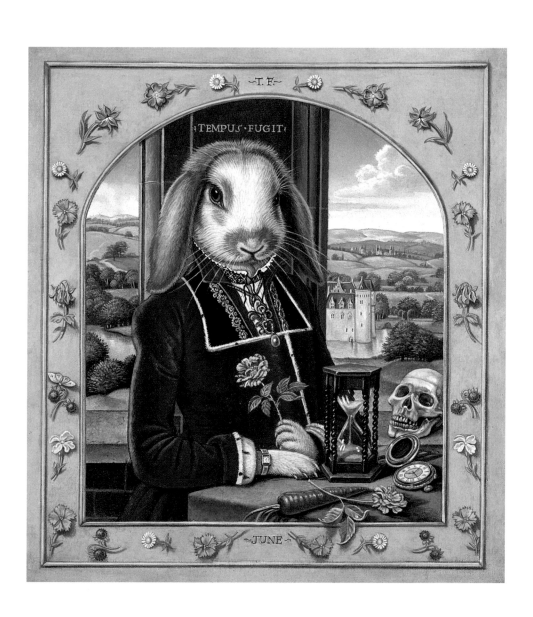

For the central figure, Fasolino refers to books in her own library, "the point being to not leave the house." For the rabbit, she needed a high-cut neckline on the dress to "finesse the connection" between the head and body. In her left hand she holds reference from a book published by the Metropolitan Museum of Art—a portrait by Jean Hey of a lady in a traditional French gown and jewelry, circa 1480-1500.
Fasolino has used Holbein reference on any number of jobs. The piece on the upper left is his "Unknown Young Man at his Office Desk," 1541, from which she "stole" the table, the collar, and the puff of one sleeve.
The borders, in her right hand, are from a book of Renaissance margin decorations from Auguste Racinet's Historic Ornament published by Dover.

She goes through her library and files to cull appropriate imagery for the job. Although she has many photographs of her rabbits from other jobs, none are in the proper pose, so she takes some 35mm shots.
In searching for a photo of a pocket watch from a previous job, she came upon some photos of a skull used for an illustration for a mystery. Aware that the image of a skull traditionally represents the passing of time in allegorical still lifes, she decides to use it in the piece. She also adds the formal phrase: Tempus Fugit: "Time Passeth."
The hourglass, which she photographed from various angles, was from Props for Today, a prop rental house.
All the reference—the different positions of the skull, all the possible watches, flower references, rabbit poses—goes into the fat job file, much of which she won't use.

To position the central figure she makes a tracing of the French portrait using an HB pencil and H for fine details.
"Tracing paper is the greatest thing ever invented; it's ideal for making additions and changes. I think with it. If I do a drawing that's not right it gets all jumbled in my head. By putting it underneath a piece of tracing paper, it clears my mind."
As for the model, it was a toss-up between Daphne, on the left, and June on the right, but because Fasolino had decided on a female costume, June's more feminine lop ears are the deciding factor.

After her initial sketch, Fasolino feels the head is too small, so she enlarges it on the Xerox in small increments (111%, 115%, 120%), then chooses the one that looks the best.

Throughout the composition, Fasolino tapes down "little patches"— drawn elements—onto the central drawing. Any changes can be redrawn and taped down. Here, to open the composition up a bit, she moves elements traced from the border reference, measuring between each one. She completes one-half then flops it to the other side and traces it.

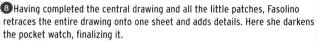

⑥ Taping the drawing of the watch. To create the curve on the wrist she draws it free-hand then flops it.

⑦ At this point, she thought she had completed the drawing, but after consideration she felt the body was too long in proportion to the head so she shortens the torso. This also leaves enough room for the type at the top.
She used the Holbein reference for the lettering of "Tempus Fugit," tracing his T and E, and making up the rest. She feels it is not perfect.
The hourglass was Xeroxed in four sizes; she then chose the one best suited to the composition.

⑧ Having completed the central drawing and all the little patches, Fasolino retraces the entire drawing onto one sheet and adds details. Here she darkens the pocket watch, finalizing it.

⑨ The finished drawing. At this point she would either fax the image to a client in two pieces or send a reduced Xerox of it. This is the stage at which the client might request changes. If there are any, only the "crazy types" would need new sketches.

⑩ She works on a 1/4-inch masonite panel, cut to size. This panel is 13- by 11 1/2-inches so it has a bleed beyond the "live" area of the illustration. With a 1 1/2-inch gesso brush she uses Liquitex Polymer Medium to "glue" double-primed linen canvas on the panel. She applies the Polymer on both the masonite and the back of the canvas. After pressing the canvas down, she rolls it out with a rubber roller, and makes deep "hospital corners" on

the back. Then she regessoes the entire surface.
Between steps 10 and 11 she applied a ground of Raw Sienna and gesso with a 2 1/2-inch gesso brush. She varies the ground depending on the job. She only uses White if the image is to be vignetted.

⑪ To transfer her drawing to the canvas, Fasolino uses Saral Transfer Paper which comes in a roll and is available in Graphite, White, Blue, Yellow, and Red.
She draws with a 7H, 8H or 9H pencil.

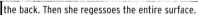

12 After shading, darkening, and refining the drawing on the canvas, she fixes it with Grumbacher Matte Tuffilm Final Fixative. Three years ago, after a career of using acrylic paints, she

took up oils and had to change some of her methods. Advice from other artists helped her considerably.

13 Her palette is a piece of glass with white cardboard beneath it. She lays out a wide range of colors—if she's working on a red dress for example, she includes even more reds.

14 Fasolino always begins with the background. The sky colors are laid out on the palette: Ultramarine Blue, Prussian Blue, Naples Yellow, Cadmium Lemon, White. She mixes five values for the sky. She uses photographic reference for the clouds which she prefers to those in the French portrait.
Her brushes are L.K. Hecht which are similar to the Winsor & Newton Series 7 brushes. She uses 000,00, 0, 1 and 2 brushes as well as the French Kolinsky Sable brush on occasion.

15 The fan brush is used to blend as she works from dark to light.

16 The background is nearly complete and corresponds to the background in the French portrait (except for the clouds), and for some small details in the landscaping, for which Fasolino used a Raphael painting for reference.
The colors for the blue hills in the distance are the same as those she used for the sky. As she moves down, she adds more greens: Viridian Green, Sap Green, Hooker's Green and White. She adds a bit of Yellow around the horizon. To the foreground she adds more Yellow, Ochre, and Green. The dark roof is a mix of Browns and Black, the other one is Mars Red, Indian Red and White. On the right, the water is bluish green as reflected from the castle. On the left it's more purple because it's next to the crimson costume.
The shadows are Sap or Hooker's Green, Burnt Sienna and Ultramarine Blue. As she goes up toward the light she adds Cadmium Green, Permanent Green Light and Yellow.
The stone behind June: the darkest is mostly Burnt Umber, a little Burnt Sienna, some Raw Umber, a little Ultramarine Blue. The lighter is Indian Red and Burnt Sienna. On the left side is Raw Sienna, White and Yellow Ochre.

17 With her reference close by, she paints the small castles. The roofs are Prussian and Ultramarine Blue. She obtains the needed values by mixing the blues with White and a tiny bit of Yellow.

18 To create the foliage on the lower left she must go over it a number of times. She began with Sap or Hooker's Green, Burnt Sienna, Burnt Umber and Ultramarine Blue. For the next value she adds White, Cadmium Green and Burnt Sienna. Then she adds White, Cadmium Green and Cadmium Yellow Pale and Yellow Ochre, then more White. The highlights are Cadmium Green, White and Cadmium Lemon.
She uses a 23-inch ruler with two erasers taped to the back to lean on as a guide and to keep her hand off the surface.

19 A detail of the wall is mostly Raw Sienna, Raw Umber, and White. Fasolino always starts working at the top with the sky. As she comes forward she adds colors. "You can't put the figure in without the background. It dictates the balance of color in the foreground."

20 Using reference, she paints the skull using Burnt Umber, a little Ivory Black, a touch of Ultramarine Blue and Raw Umber. She adds White and a little Burnt Sienna and Raw Sienna. Then more White. The shadows and reflected light are Ultramarine Blue with White, as is the highlight.

21 Now she lays out the reds for the gown: Alizarin Crimson, Winsor Violet, Permanent Rose, Bright Red, Scarlet Red, and, of course, White. She mixes five values to start. The shadows are Alizarin Crimson, a little Winsor Violet and Burnt Umber. She adds White and Permanent Rose, Alizarin Crimson and Bright Red. Then Scarlet Red and White for the lighter value. She uses a fan brush to soften the gradations.

22 An older, more worn brush is effective in softening the edges in the shadows. The velvety look is achieved by making the middle passage on the sleeve quite dark with the edges being much lighter. As is evident in the reference, the velvet pile picks up light. She uses White and a bit of Yellow on the lightest part of the sleeve, and keeps the right-hand side cooler by using Permanent Rose. Scarlet Red warms up the left. It's important to introduce not just light and dark into the picture, but warm and cool as well.

23 Mixing up a glaze on a paper palette. Her glaze medium is traditional: 1/3 linseed oil, 1/3 damar varnish, 1/3 English distilled varnish with a drop of Cobalt drier, which allows the glaze to dry in a couple of hours.
She mixes the glaze to give some warmth to the sky. First she mixes Viridian Green and Permanent Green Light. Then she mixes Indian Yellow and Permanent Rose for an orange, which she adds to the green glaze.
It is important to note that after painting and before varnishing, Fasolino will often use a retouch spray varnish (a damar varnish) on the painting. This is used to isolate the layers of paint, and lessen the absorbancy of the ground or layers. Because it separates the layers, it also allows for changes in case she is not pleased with the glaze. If changes are needed, the glazes can be wiped off using cheese cloth before they set. The spray varnish also brings out a uniform wetness throughout.

24 To carry down the glaze she uses a badger brush blender. Because it "has all these little points it gives an airbrush effect."

21

22

23

24

(25) The yoke of the dress is Black, Ultramarine Blue, Prussian Blue and Burnt Umber. Often the deep blacks pop out and look like a "hole," so Fasolino lightens it with White, blues and browns. Here she paints Black around the jewelry using a 00 brush.

(26) She starts painting the eye using Ivory Black, Burnt Umber and Raw Umber together, then lightens it with a bit of White. Three values of these colors are used for the eyeball and socket.

(27) This is really close work and because she's using oil as her medium which requires a longer drying time, Fasolino's paintings have gotten smaller. To aid her vision she uses an Optivisor, a magnifying device used by jewelers. Here she is surrounded by bunny pictures.

(28) To create the bunny fur she uses White and Raw Sienna for the lightest areas. She adds more Raw Sienna and Raw Umber and a touch of Prussian or Cerulean Blue for the darker areas. She then applies a glaze of Raw Sienna and Burnt Sienna.
She goes back and builds up the whites. To get more pink around the nose she uses Permanent Rose, Light Flesh, and Deep Flesh, then adds an Alizarin Crimson glaze over the nose. Around the eyes she adds some pink and a few highlights.

----

(29) The watch case begins with earth colors: Burnt Umber, Raw Umber, Winsor Violet and a little Ivory Black. The lighter areas are Raw Sienna, Yellow Ochre and White. She adds more White, Cadmium Lemon, Cadmium Yellow Pale, and Chrome Yellow to brighten the gold.
Because Yellows always need building up, she glazes over the watch case several times. She only has the patience to make five values, so she must "make up for it by using the glazes."

(30) The shadows of the pearl are Burnt and Raw Umber, the middle area is White, and White and Ultramarine Blue for reflected light. She glazes over the pearl to darken it a bit. Here she paints in the highlight again, over the glaze.
The ermine is Burnt Umber, Raw Umber in the shadow, and a bit of reflected red. She gets the texture by using little brush strokes.

28

29

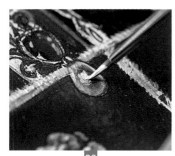

30

31 Using all the Yellows in five values she copies her reference photo of the wrist watch. To get a darker tone, she uses a glaze, then builds up the highlights using White over the glaze.

32 Fasolino had blooms from a Tudor Rose bush in her country house garden. As a very old, striped variety, she felt it appropriate to the era. The colors are basically the same as in the gown.

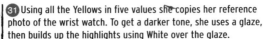

33 She had included a carrot in the still life she'd photographed with the hourglass. The highlight is White, Cadmium Orange and Cadmium Yellow Pale. The next value is Cadmium Orange with less White. Then Burnt Sienna, Mars Red and a purple. For the darker area she adds Burnt Umber, Burnt Sienna and Purple. She glazes it over with Scarlet Red to keep it from looking a bit powdery or chalky.
The shadows in the stem are browns, the lighter part is Cadmium Yellow, Cadmium Green and White.

34 For the table she's mixed five values, as always: the deepest shadow is Viridian Green, Burnt Umber and a touch of Ultramarine Blue. The second shadow in a middle tone is White, Viridian, Cadmium Green, and a bit of Burnt Umber. The lighter area is White, Cadmium Green, Cadmium Yellow Pale, Cadmium Lemon and a little Ochre. After glazing, she highlights with White.

35 After she took the photos of her rented, empty hourglass, she thought that sand should have been falling through, so she had to make it up. She added more highlights so it would "come away from the sleeve," which she had lightened. The wood is Burnt Umber, Raw Umber, Black, a touch of Alizarin Crimson and Ultramarine Blue. The wood grain is White with Ochre, a touch of Burnt Sienna, and a little red. She drags the brush through the brown for the grain effect.

36 To create the border she begins with a wash of Red Oxide. On top she mixes Yellow Ochre and White and adds a touch of Metallic Gold paint. To get rules she uses her ruler guide like a dowel stick, tipping her hand and brush against it at a 45% angle.
After painting in the flowers from reference, she deepens the shadows and completes the highlighting. She applies an Indian Yellow glaze in certain spots because on a frame some places shine out more brightly.

37 She does the lettering last, using some of the Gold paint. Because it doesn't stand out enough, she goes over it again with Yellow and White. Once the border is finished, she glazes down the stone sill a tone because it was too similar in value to the border.
Fasolino always has the work photographed: an 8 by 10 transparency as a record and sample, and 35mm slides for lectures and competitions. She builds a foamcore and cardboard box to size and uses FedEx for out-of-town clients. She'll see clients herself or send the work by messenger if they're in the city.
Fasolino is rarely asked to make changes on the final painting. Her agent keeps tabs on any changes requested from a final that's been created from an approved sketch. The client is charged for these changes.

left: "The Christmas Cat," Berkley Publishing, Joni Friedman, Art Director, right: "Rabbit with Paint Brush," School of Visual Arts, Silas Rhodes, Art Director

"Cows in Meadow," Pintail Design Ltd, Simon Dear, Art Director

66
teresa
fasolino

"Scales of Justice," Berkley Publishing, Joni Friedman, Art Director

teresa
fasolino

top: "Noah's Ark," Poppe Tyson for Drew Industries, Bill Kopp, Art Director
bottom: "Adam & Eve," BMP/DDB Needham for Finsons, Peter Gatley, Art Director

top: "Dueling Knights," Garrison Lontine for Watneys Beer, Clarice Bonzer, Art Director
bottom: "St. George and the Dragon," Pennette & Partners for Loop-Lock, Mike Pennette, Art Director

teresa
fasolino

"Picnic Scene with Fruit Basket," Grand Union, Milton Glaser, Art Director

"The Sophisticated Traveler," *The New York Times*, Nicki Kalish, Art Director

Teresa Fasolino attended the School of Visual Arts where she studied with Robert Weaver, and Marshall Arisman, among others. She has worked for most major magazines, publishers, and advertising agencies, evolving and developing her particular and recognizable style of illustrative painting. In addition to working in the print media, she has worked with architects and interior designers to create paintings for restaurants at The World Trade Center and an eight-foot mural for the Trattoria Dellarte restaurant in New York. Some of her clients include the United States Postal Service, *The New York Times Magazine*, *Berkley Publishing*, and Pfizer Pharmaceuticals. Her work has been exhibited numerous times at the Society of Illustrators and various New York galleries. She teaches a course in painting for illustrators at the School of Visual Arts.

MARK HESS'S BOYISH EXUBERANCE IS REFLECTED IN HIS CLASSIC 1956 WHITE CORVETTE WITH RED LEATHER INTERIOR WHICH MAKES SHORT WORK OF THE CURVING WOODED ROADS LEADING TO HIS CHARMING HOUSE AN HOUR NORTH OF NEW YORK CITY. HE'S AMBIVALENT ABOUT BEING THE SON OF LEGENDARY ILLUSTRATOR DICK HESS—GRATEFUL FOR HIS ARTISTIC GIFTS, UNEASY IN THE LONG SHADOW OF HIS FATHER'S REPUTATION. HESS'S STUDIO IS FILLED WITH BOOKS, STACKED PAINTINGS, A STUFFED OWL, AND A VARIETY OF MASKS AND ANIMAL SKULLS. WHEN TALKING TO A CLIENT, HESS HAS A BARRAGE OF QUESTIONS FOR THE ART DIRECTOR: "TELL ME ABOUT YOUR BUSINESS. TELL ME ABOUT YOUR SUCCESSES IN THE PAST. TELL ME ABOUT YOUR ADVERTISING. WHAT'S YOUR TARGET AUDIENCE? WHAT DO YOU THINK your voice is? Are you an innovative company that wants to emulate Swatch or are you Upper Class?" To Hess, understanding the client's business and how they want to represent themselves is the most important part of the job, more important than coming up with the concept.

After discussing a company's needs, Hess goes through old graphics annuals researching the ad campaigns of other similar companies. He wants to see work that's been judged by his peers, to see what the client's competition does successfully. Also, for certain jobs, if there has been television advertising, he reviews commercials at the Museum of TV and Radio.

He then comes back to the client, either the CEO or the creative director at the agency.

It's uncommon for an agency to give him an open-ended assignment these days. "They've gone through layers of executives, so that by the time the illustrator is hired, they'll have sketches or one or two comprehensives, or "comps," a layout showing the elements of the ad. Often they've seen something in an illustrator's portfolio that relates to their own concept: `We need a cliff painting. You've done a cliff.' They know what they'll get."

Hess finds that with a new client you may be miscast. Sometimes they are surprised and disappointed. That's why it's so important to get to know what the client thinks they're all about. It allows you to fulfill their expectations." He doesn't just want to be a "hired hand." He wants it to succeed for the "whole gestalt." It helps for getting hired again.

"Fewer and fewer art directors think they can collaborate with the illustrator and not simply assign a job. Because there are a lot of marketing people—too many cooks mixing the stew—there's no strong thrust. Even the legendary art directors,

those with a powerful vision, can't act as they used to. The reality is clients think they know more than the experts they hire."

After we had discussed this "Time" assignment, Hess imagined a big watch company with many different brands, trying to shock people into reading their headline: "Time is on your side." They wouldn't say anything about the product in the image itself ("Let's face it, all watches are accurate these days"), but they'd be trying to get you to realize they were a brand apart from the other companies. They wouldn't be doing hard marketing of a particular watch; they'd be talking about the importance of time in a person's life.

1 Hess feels that painting is not his strongest skill. He's not "cutting edge," or particularly individualistic. But he brings to the table a strong conceptual sense and a strong desire to communicate what the client wants.

He works on sketches that don't show product. Normally, at this stage, he would try to talk to the client on the phone, checking back and forth as ideas come to him. He loves to collaborate.

1a Hess first searches through a variety of sources, including many annuals of illustration. This gets him into the "inspiration mode" for ideas, not specific images. Under the heading "Watch Company," he writes phrases that are appropriate to the subject matter: "Time as friend. Time helping. Past disappearing. Time is a mystery."

He starts visualizing in 1- by 1-inch thumbnail sketches. Generally, they are NOT in proportion at this stage, but act as "snapshots." Because the drawings are so rough, he puts a written description beneath each one. Under these thumbnails he has written: "watch across chasm, drawbridge clock, clock hand crossing chasm, stairway burning, dark sky–bright cloudy clock, watch doorway to Eden-like landscape." He'll go back and canni-

balize from some or all of these sketches for his final idea.

The overall idea is of an image of a large clock which "represents time in your life." The small figures represent Everyman. It's a conceptual style he has used over the years: "the little guy presented with some obstacle that he must overcome."

2 Hess leaves the piece for a day, works on other projects and clears his mind. He returns fresh and "surprises himself" with the sketches. He picks one (in this case the one on the left), cuts it out, triples its size in the Xerox, then faxes it to the client. On a real job, he includes a written description to help the art director when he or she shows the image to others in the organization who may not be visually trained. Any changes to the concept and layout are discussed at this point.

3 He stretches primed "cheap cotton canvas." He has tried higher grade linen canvas but it didn't affect his work either way, so he uses the less costly material. He sands the surface lightly to remove any irregularities.

4 With a 6-inch spackle knife he applies acrylic Raw Umber from the tube for a dark neutral ground. Two coats of paint makes a good ground to show his chalk transfer (see Step 10).

5 With a staple gun he affixes the dry canvas to the stretchers.

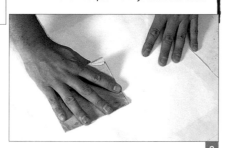

6

6

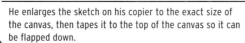

He enlarges the sketch on his copier to the exact size of the canvas, then tapes it to the top of the canvas so it can be flapped down.

7

He covers one side of a piece of tracing paper with plain white blackboard chalk.

8

He puts the transfer sheet under the sketch and traces the drawing using a #2 pencil, leaving a chalk impression on the ground.

9

He lifts the sketch to check the drawing on the canvas.

10

The traced sketch on the canvas.

11

Hess mixes the color for the sky: Cobalt Blue, Ultramarine Blue, Pthalocyanine Blue, White, Yellow Oxide and Turner's Yellow. For the sky he mixes five or six "puddles" of paint, using a variety of brands. The French FlashÇ brand he finds to be more opaque and covers better. He mixes only as much as he thinks he'll need for the moment.
He uses a strip palette and keeps his paints in a plastic fishing tackle box where they can stay fresh for months. For most work he uses Winsor & Newton Series 7 brushes, almost all 00 or 0. For scumbling he uses Winsor & Newton Series 233 or any other natural bristle pointed brush. On occasion, he likes a filbert.

11

10

9

8

12

In this case, Hess applies the sky by painting from light to dark, though he sometimes paints from dark to light—it depends on the piece. It takes three coats to get the sky colors to blend "decently." One of his tricks is to use clouds to cover imperfect blends.

13 Drying the area with a lamp.

14 He uses his fingers to blend the pigment.

15 Before painting in the clouds, he re-emphasizes the clock hands to insure they will not be obscured. To get a hard-edged line he traces the clock hand with the aid of a ruler.

To keep his paints moist, he puts down five layers of wet paper towels in the air-tight fishing tackle box. He uses a full palette, regardless of the overall color scheme. "Don't exclude the possibility of using any color. Sometimes you want to put green in a shadow. You can get tied up using only two or three colors."

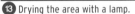

16

He draws in the clouds with chalk, creating his overall pattern. He uses chalk because pencil is greasy and the chalk can be absorbed by the paint later.

Does he use reference for the clouds? "Everyone uses reference, whether they know it or not." With his experience, Hess doesn't need physical reference in front of him because "I have an encyclopedia inside my head." He has looked closely and carefully at enough clouds, and, he notes, he can go outside and look up if he needs to.

The best reference, Hess contends, is the interpretation of other painters—Magritte, for instance. He is not interested in "getting reality down right." He's aiming at "a simplistic intellectualization of what reality is. I don't want to `wow' people with technical prowess—I want to speak to them from a more friendly, untutored stance."

Here he uses a compass to describe the chalk outline of the clock face.

For the clouds he uses Titanium White, Yellow Oxide, Turner's Yellow and Cadmium Red Light.

He pats the color with his fingers to make the cloud shapes. At the same time, the chalk sketch beneath is absorbed.

The clock face on the original sketch is quite rough. Referring to a clock he has in the studio, which can be seen in Step 30, Hess traces a more refined drawing over the sketch.

Using acrylic paint in a ruling pen compass, he describes a very thin line over the dry background.

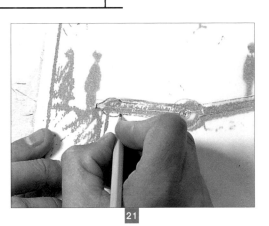

He draws freehand over the ruling pen line to create a "squiggly," more hand-painted look to the line. "If the clock looked mechanically done, everything else would have to and I don't know how to do the rest of it!"

Because cliffs are made out of rocks, Hess begins by visualizing rocks. He wants to make them a little warmer than the Raw Umber ground in contrast to the cool blue of the sky. Again, having created cliffs before, the reference is in his head. But he points out that he can refer to his huge picture file if necessary. If he doesn't know how a thing looks, he takes Polaroids—for particular hand shapes or people's stances, for example. This painting is supposed to be "simplistic and strange, on a mind plane, a dream."

He keeps playing with the cliffs. He adds Burnt Umber and Black to the original Raw Umber ground. He tightens up the edges, discovers little ridges and creates highlights. He works one side until he feels "something good is happening. I don't think, I just do. I'm not conscious of what goes into it at the time."

His palette at this stage: Burnt Umber, Burnt Sienna, Yellow and Red Oxide, Turner's Yellow, Dioxazine Purple. He makes his own purple by mixing Cadmium Red, Ultramarine Blue and Cobalt Blue.

 For straight lines, he runs the ferrule of the brush against an 18-inch steel rule tilted up on one edge.

He decides to make the clock hands gold using Yellow Orange Oxide, Raw Sienna, Cadmium Light and White. To achieve the "weird patterns of light on metal," he "just tried something," to get the proper highlight. It's a combination of White and Yellow Orange Oxide which he blends out. As he generally works from dark to light, the hands went in dark and he built up the lights.

Hess wants to make clear that he creates colors off his palette "by instinct." In other words, he might create another pair of gold clock hands with similar, but not necessarily exactly the same colors he used here. He may just pull a color from a "wet puddle" that happens to be there. With enough experience, a certain randomness is part of the process.

Though Hess used reference for some of the people, none are an exact replica. These people are not photographically "real," rather, they are indications of "types of people." He uses reference for the correct placement of a man's hand on his thigh in relation to the end of his suit jacket. The figure on the right happens to be Dick Clarke, the rock 'n roll empressario. Hess uses the shape of Clarke's hair in one of the figures.

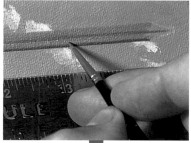

29 Hess checks his reference to see if the man's shirt is visible or just the tie. Then he starts "pushing the paint around." Sometimes it goes quickly, sometimes it comes together, and sometimes he has to repaint things six times.

30 At first, Hess tried putting the numerals down in chalk. But to get a distinct font at such a small size, he found he needed to draw each one in pencil. (The cloud reference on the left-hand side of his board happened to be there from a job he did two years ago.)

31 He draws one numeral at a time then paints it. After the paint dries (in about fifteen seconds), he erases the pencil lines. He says, "The people stand safely on the metal hands, hence they are very concrete in their look. But the numerals are dreams—transparent in a way."

32 While considering if he's satisfied with the size and proportion of the numerals, he takes a break and goes to work on the flowers. He feels the landscape should be more enticing on the right-hand cliff, where the figures are heading on their journey through time.

To finish the piece he lightens up the cliffs by adding more White and Yellow to the original palette (see Step 25). He completes the numerals using the same pencil-to-paint technique. In the process, he changes the position of the numeral 3 and re-paints it. All the numerals are darkened slightly and the highlights brightened so they stand out more strikingly. He adds a tree on the right-hand cliff, again using his internal imagination as reference. He adds the other characters. Because he feels unsure about the audience, he's hesitant about who should be represented. He decides to tailor it for business people, so there are no children, no one in a leisure suit. In a real job he would have discussed the political correctness of the figures in advance. Would they want a Latino? A handicapped person? And in what order should the women and men appear? Is the woman's dress above or below her knees? Who holds the briefcase? These kinds of discussions have become very important in advertising and corporate assignments.

At the very end he varnishes the picture using 50% Liquitex Matte Varnish and 50% Gloss Medium and Varnish to which he adds 10% water. The consistency is like heavy cream. He gives a uniform coating with a 1-inch natural bristle brush using quick and even horizontal strokes. He blows out all the little bubbles.

"Today, scanners see EVERYTHING, each tooth of the canvas is reflected. The technical expertise of the scanner operator is crucial to the outcome of the printing job." Over the years, Hess has "matted down" his technique, which is helpful when scanning the image, but it can flatten out the work. "Varnish juices everything up. Darks are darker and lights are shinier and brighter."

Before sending the work out, Hess photographs it in his studio to avoid having to re-do a job if the art should get lost. Also, photos are good for slide presentations. He uses tungsten film and lights in his "fairly professional set-up."

Because varnish liquifies at 95 degrees Fahrenheit, he puts a protective piece of waxed paper between the painting and a tracing paper cover sheet.

Hess always includes a "nice warm note" that says, "Give me a call so I don't worry." He feels it's important to always maintain a sense of humor and a sense of humanity. For the client, it connects the job to a human being.

If there are changes desired by the client after they see the piece, Hess will make them after some debate, but he must be convinced. He will negotiate a price for substantial changes.

29

30

31

32

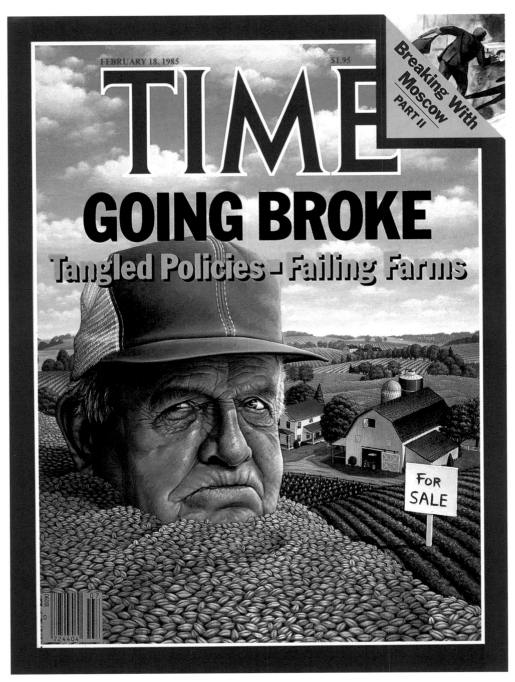

"Broke Farmers," *Time*, Rudy Hoglund, Art Director

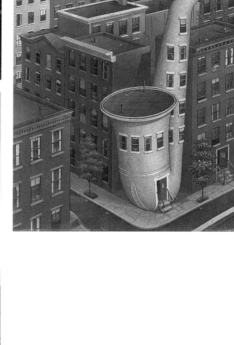

top: "The Republicans are Coming," *Newsweek*, Candy Litrell, Art Director
bottom: "Vane Pursuit," Warner Books, Jackie Merri Meyer, Art Director
right: "Sax Building," Columbia, Gene Greit, Art Director

"Legends of the West," United States Postal Service, Dick Sheaff, Art Director

"Cat Fantastic," Daw Books, Sheila Gilbert, Art Director

"Middle Passage," Macmillan Books, Wendy Bass, Art Director

Original.   Chunky.

Whether you choose our original sauce with imported olive oil
and romano cheese, or our chunky homestyle with bits of tomato,
herbs and spices, you'll get classic Italian taste.

PRINCE

**If all the books in the Library of Congress
were books, it could take you
twelve miles to get from A to Z.**

If the information stored in the Library of Congress were allowed to grow ungoverned, it would take over the Government. But thanks to microfilm, those records can be shrunk dramatically and then retrieved in record time.

As a pioneer in the microfilm industry, 3M has been hearing about the mounting problems of storing, filing and retrieving information for years.

Because at 3M, we're in the business of hearing.

By listening to people's needs, we've kept ahead of the information explosion with new ideas and advances in microfilm technology like the highly efficient 3M "Micrapoint" Filing System.

In fact, 3M has pioneered over 700 products for the office, training and business field alone.

If you think you might have an application for our technologies and products write us today for a free 3M Office, Training and Business Brochure. Department 060205/ 3M, P.O. Box 4039, St. Paul, MN 55104.

Or better yet, let us hear from you right now. Call toll-free: 1-800-323-1718, Operator 366. (Illinois Residents call 1-800-942-8881)

3M hears you....

3M

top: "Original or Chunky," Prince, Al Scully, Art Director, bottom: "Wide Washington," 3M, Bill Monahan, Art Director

"Building Money," *Gordons Magazine*, Dick Hess, Art Director

"Living in the Shadow of Industry," *Fortune*, Margery Peters, Art Director

87
mark
hess

Raised in Michigan, Mark Hess became a professional bull rider at the age of ten, then attended
the University of Colorado where he majored in Fine Arts and graduated in 1972. He began his
illustration career in 1975 and received his first New York Art Directors Club Gold medal in 1976.
Since then, Hess has appeared in many graphics journals and won awards from The New York
One Show; the Detroit, Miami, Connecticut, Los Angeles, Chicago and San Francisco Art Directors
Clubs; the Boston Creative Show; and Catholic Press Association, among others. His work has
been exhibited at the Georges Pompidou Museum in Paris and is held in the permanent
collections of The Museum of Natural History in New York
and The Smithsonian Institution, Washington, D.C., as well as in private collections.
His clients include: *Time*, *Newsweek*, *Forbes*, IBM, Xerox, 3M, CBS, ABC, Levi-Strauss, Champion
International, Coors, Budweiser, Heineken, American Express, MasterCard, Mobil, *The New York
Times*, *Esquire*, *Business Week*, *Playboy*, *Rolling Stone*, *TV Guide*, *Sports Illustrated*, AT&T,
Random House, Simon & Schuster, Warner Communications, Knopf, Paramount, and the U.S.

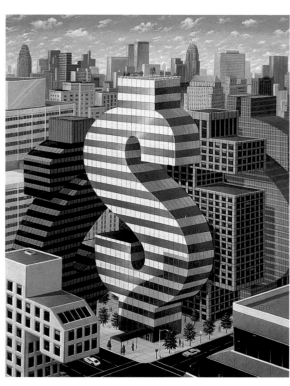

"Building Money," *Gordons Magazine*, Dick Hess, Art Director

"Living in the Shadow of Industry," *Fortune*, Margery Peters, Art Director

HERBIE MANN • GERRY MULLIGAN • EARLE WARREN   JAY McSHANN THE BIG APPLE BASH   DOC CHEATHAM • DICKY WELLS • JOHN SCOFIELD
EDDIE GOMEZ • MILT HINTON • JACK SIX • CONNIE KAY   JOE MORELLO • SAMMY FIGUEROA • JANIS SIEGEL

Raised in Michigan, Mark Hess became a professional bull rider at the age of ten, then attended
the University of Colorado where he majored in Fine Arts and graduated in 1972. He began his
illustration career in 1975 and received his first New York Art Directors Club Gold medal in 1976.
Since then, Hess has appeared in many graphics journals and won awards from The New York
One Show; the Detroit, Miami, Connecticut, Los Angeles, Chicago and San Francisco Art Directors
Clubs; the Boston Creative Show; and Catholic Press Association, among others. His work has
been exhibited at the Georges Pompidou Museum in Paris and is held in the permanent
collections of The Museum of Natural History in New York
and The Smithsonian Institution, Washington, D.C., as well as in private collections.
His clients include: *Time*, *Newsweek*, *Forbes*, IBM, Xerox, 3M, CBS, ABC, Levi-Strauss, Champion
International, Coors, Budweiser, Heineken, American Express, MasterCard, Mobil, *The New York
Times*, *Esquire*, *Business Week*, *Playboy*, *Rolling Stone*, *TV Guide*, *Sports Illustrated*, AT&T,
Random House, Simon & Schuster, Warner Communications, Knopf, Paramount, and the U.S.
Postal Service for whom he has done 46 award-winning stamps.

BECAUSE MUSIC IS VERY
IMPORTANT TO THE ARTIST, A
LARGE PORTION OF HIRO'S STUDIO IS
DEVOTED TO AUDIO EQUIPMENT AND
RECORDINGS. HE WORKS AT AN
ITALIAN ARNAL DRAWING TABLE WITH
TWO LUXO LAMPS TO ILLUMINATE HIS
METICULOUS WORK. PHOTOGRAPHS
OF ELLA FITZGERALD AND OTHER
JAZZ FIGURES HANG ON THE WALLS.
HIS ART IS ALL AROUND THE HOUSE.
HE AND IKUKO, HIS WIFE OF
TWENTY YEARS, SHARE ON A QUIET
SHADY STREET IN BROOKLYN.

After getting this assignment Hiro looks in the dictionary and simply copies down the definition of Time. "This is so I have a wider view of the subject. I try to look at the problem as objectively as possible, rather than a personal notion." When pressed as to what his personal view of Time is, he says he sees it "as a river just flowing, a flow of time," noting that he believes in reincarna-tion, "without big religious overtones." He quickly decided this personal view is not what the assignment required.

He goes back to the objective consideration of Time. "First, Time equals History. So I thought: how about an historical figure in a river of time? Just a crazy notion, but that's how my ideas go. The time the watch tells you is connected to what went on in the past, to history." He come up with a swirling design to indicate the flow of time, but decided that an overall vision of history was too grandiose. "But why not personal history? This watch is for keeps, it shares your lifetime."

1 Hiro's first thumbnail sketches show his initial concepts. On the right he's indicated historical figures and in the foreground is his personal history from birth to marriage. What remained of these ideas in the final piece is only the swirling design indicated in the historical sketch.

2 As he refines his ideas, he sketches with a Rembrandt Polycolor Peacock Blue pencil and sharpens it down to the nub with a M cro NT Cutter D 400.
"I have always been interested in the image of the staircase, of things going to other levels. I thought of a lady going down a spiral staircase with her high heels clicking like the ticking of a watch. She is not in a hurry, she takes her time and she's making the man at the bottom of the stairs wait for her." Hiro also wondered, "What is the best part about having a watch? When you're waiting for someone you're really longing for and looking at the watch...that sweet moment of waiting."

3 He submits a number of sketches to a client. Then he shows Xeroxes of the sketches, marking his own order of preference. Because the customer's satisfaction is important, he hates to give the client too few choices and only submits ideas he'd be happy to work on. When I recieved his sketches for the "Time" assignment, we found that we both preferred the same one.

4 He Xeroxes the sketch in various sizes. Unless asked to do otherwise, he chooses a size that's comfortable for him to paint in.

5 Because the staircase reference he discovered didn't satisfy him in terms of lighting, he makes a model by cutting two identical paper arcs. He affixes the steps with Elmer's Glue. He had considered adding a fancy railing, but the simple shape satisfied him so much he left it as it was. "It's timeless rather than Baroque." He took crude Polaroids as reference, but he also lit it properly and simply held it up and looked at. it "Observe, memorize, paint."

6 The reference shots of the woman are of his wife Ikuko, "as usual." He's after "the lighting and shade, how it covers her face, falls on her clothing." Ikuko takes reference Polaroids of Hiro checking his watch.

7 Every reference he might need goes into a pile which is reduced as he works. Ideas come from all kinds of sources: the zebra idea came from reference for a different job—zebra chairs in a Art Deco room. From his files he takes a reproduction of a George Stubbs painting of the animal.

He draws the various segments on tracing paper with a .03 millimeter mechanical pencil, which has the same effect as a 2H pencil sharpened with a knife.
The Atlas is a design element as well as a joke: "Man carries the burden of the world as woman saunters down the staircase." The Empire State Building reference is a photo taken some time ago.

9 For the staircase, he starts with a rough sketch then, referring to the Polaroid, he makes corrections using French Curves and "C Thru" Ships Curves, templates used in nautical design. It was the hardest part of the whole piece and had to be done several times.
It was necessary to keep the balance between an "isometric" staircase (one hanging in space) and one seen in regular perspective. "Isometrically," it would look only like radiating lines, so he must add some perspective to make it clear that the woman is standing on steps that could actually hold her.

10 This tracing of his hand is a combination of three Polaroids attained by using the Lucigraph, an optical machine for making enlargements or reductions of opaque images.
He makes one element of the illustration per sheet of tracing paper, then combines them to make one complete drawing upon which he makes final adjustments.

11 Using registration marks with a ruler to help him line up all the elements exactly, he places the drawing of the woman over the staircase drawing. He prefers the Berol Verithin Rose pencil because it has less wax than Prismacolor, so the tip doesn't flatten easily. On the other hand, the Prismacolor pencils, because of their wax content, adhere better to the painting surface.

12 Using a mechanical pencil (a Graph 1000 for Pro .03 Pentel), Hiro makes the final transfer of all elements exactly to size onto tracing paper. Some art directors want to see the piece at this stage, though he is rarely asked to make changes.

13 For a rough color sketch, Hiro makes a 50% reduced Xerox of the finished drawing. He prefers British Derwent Studio pencils, and Berol and Prismacolor for the colors not available from Derwent. He keeps his pencils in a handmade, styrofoam rack. "The way I use color is lopsided—it's not how others see. I can look at objects as color shapes. For the side of the building, someone else might see a naturalistic stone color. I see pink. Usually I see it in color shape. The two things I felt I was weak in when I was a student were color and design. They turned out to be my strengths."

14

The finished color sketch.

To prepare a transfer sheet he spreads lighter fluid over pastel rubbed on tracing paper. It's taped down flat and left to dry, then wiped clean of excess. The pastel transfer line is easy to erase on the artwork. Any color pastel can be used and the transfer sheets can be used repeatedly. Hiro has had some for ten years.

Between Steps 15 and 16 he has put down a basic ground made by mixing a lot of White, Raw Umber, a touch of Dioxazine Purple, and Raw Sienna. This he refers to as "stone grey."

16 Hiro works on Crescent board, Linetex (a discontinued line), or stretched 2- or 3-ply Strathmore. It's gessoed and sanded down. Here he registers the drawing.

Transferring the drawing using a 9H pencil. **17**

18 He places tracing paper over the entire drawing, then cuts out the area he's going to work on. Working shape by shape, he puts down Grapfix Prepared Frisket which he gets directly from the manufacturer. Here he cuts out the woman's dress.

19 He filters the paint with a stocking because acrylic paint tends to harden and clog the airbrush. After trying many kinds of airbrushes, he favors his Olympus Airbrush HP 100C.

He prefers Golden paints from jars and Liquitex paints from the tube. He premixes his colors and puts a portion on a wax palette. He thins the pigment with water to a 50/50 consistency. The acrylic paints dry in 10 minutes.

20 The dress is "just flat airbrushing," using a mix of Dioxazine Purple, Acra Violet, and a touch of Burnt Umber.

Proper ventilation is absolutely necessary. Hiro uses a double-barrelled respirator. He warns that the "Cadmium colors never leave the body and that they are carcinogenic."

15

16

14

17

18

19

20

21 Hiro puts his premixed colors in jars. He labels and refrigerates them; he says they last for years!

22 Lifting the frisket. The colors for the pink building are Pyrrole Red, a bit of Raw Umber, and White. The yellow building is Raw Umber and White. He adds Dioxazine Purple for the darker shapes. The burgundy circles which will be wine glasses are of Acra Violet, a touch of Dioxazine Purple, plus Burnt Umber.

23 To make the airbrush texture more interesting Hiro employs a toothbrush to splatter the paint. "Everything I learned about art, I learned in kindergarten," he laughs.

24 The rudimentary background and woman's figure are complete. Her hat is a mixture of Burnt Umber and Pthalo Blue because Black from the tube is too flat. The round, Guggenheim-shaped building is Raw Sienna, Dioxazine Purple, and White.

25 He makes an acetate frisket of the general shape of the shaded area on the staircase. He airbrushes very lightly using Pthalo Blue, White, Dioxazine Purple, and a touch of Raw Sienna to soften it.

26 Without frisket Hiro refines the shapes and extends the lines. He introduces the medium tone, making variations by the amount of paint he uses: more paint deepens the hue. He establishes the middle and dark tones.

27 He has added many elements to the picture at this point: The sky is Brilliant Blue, Purple, White, and a touch of Dioxazine Purple. The clouds are Turquoise Green, White, and a touch of Yellow Oxide, with just a touch of Dioxazine Purple (one of Hiro's favorite colors). The wine bottle is Burnt Umber and Dioxazine Purple. Its large label is Raw Sienna and White with a touch of Acra Violet, and the small label is a mix of the sky color with a touch of Pthalo Blue. The man's sleeve is Pthalo Blue and Dioxazine Purple. The base color of his watch is White, Black, Dioxazine Purple, and a touch of Raw Sienna.
To create the flesh tone for the man's hands he divides the pigment into four or five tones, starting with the medium tone: Pyrrole Red, White, and a touch of Yellow. The dark tone is Pyrrole Red and Burnt Umber, and the darkest tone is Burnt Umber and Red Violet. The light tone is Pyrrole Red with more White and more Yellow.

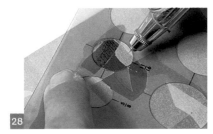
28

29

30

31

32

28

To shade the woman's face he uses a circle template for convenience. He'll come
back later to paint in the details and add
more subtle shading.

29

Hiro has applied the darkest overall tone
on the Atlas in Turquoise Green,
Dioxazine Purple, and White. Now he puts
a transfer sheet between the final tracing paper drawing and the airbrushed
surface. After making certain it's registered,
he draws in the tight details. He will then draw
the Atlas in a blue colored pencil over the pastel transfer lines.

30 Most details are done freehand using
Winsor & Newton brushes. He mixes the base
color of Turquoise Green plus a touch of White.
He goes over the pencilled-in details with a 00
brush in a handmade bamboo holder. It keeps
the ache in his hand at a minimum, since hold-
ing a narrow brush for hours can be painful.
After the basic modeling is done he erases the
unnecessary transfer lines.

31 He has put the mid-tone down on the Atlas
and now comes in with a lighter tone. This is
the look Hiro is known for: the flatness of airbrush with the dimensional feel of the
unblended light tone on top.

32 As in Step 29, he transfers the details onto
the staircase using a ruler and a 9H pencil.

33 Painting in the risers of the steps with a
00 brush using the basic "stone color" (see
paragraph after Step 15). He calls it "swirling."

34 He holds the staircase model as lighting
reference.

34

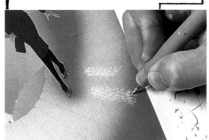
33

35

With a ruling pen tipped at a slight angle, he draws in the edges of the steps.

36 He "swirls" around the woman's shadow.

37 He touches up the gaps where the frisket left unclean lines. The shoes, which are Pyrrole Red with a touch of Dioxazine Purple, he paints with a brush, not the airbrush. Hiro claims he's terrible at laying down large areas of flat color with a brush, so the airbrush solves that problem. But for small areas he prefers to do it by hand. He likes the combination of the flat airbrushed areas and the feel of drawing in the hand-painted details.

36

38 At this point all areas have at least a base color.
He airbrushed the windows three rows at a time. The grey windows in the pink building on the left are White, Black, Dioxazine Purple, and a touch of Raw Sienna. The windows of the pink building on the right are the same color as the bottle label. The windows in the yellow building, third from left, are the middle tone of the deep Atlas color mixed with a touch of the medium tone.

38

Using the same methods throughout, Hiro completes the piece. The watch face is White, Dioxazine Purple, a touch of Black, and a touch of Pthalo Blue. He renders the watch tightly but not photographically. To make it look expensive he adds more details. The gold ring around the face balances with Atlas's world and the shape of the wine glasses.

Throughout, Hiro is very careful how he mixes colors and their relative values. It is important in keeping the connections within the painting clear—it somehow tightens it up. Otherwise "you can go all over the place." This is especially true in this piece with its strong central shape. "You don't want the elements on the periphery to fly off; it's the color that keeps them connected." By using the main colors (such as the deep purple of the shadow on the stairs or the middle tone of the Atlas color) in other shapes, the viewer is "taken all around the picture plane."

It takes him about two days to complete the drawing, including coming up with ideas, gathering reference and shooting the Polaroids. The airbrushing takes about a day- and-a-half to two days. By the end of the fourth day he's got a finish.

He puts on his one-name signature using Futura Bold press type.

To transport the picture he tapes it on foamcore with an acetate overlay and a grey construction paper cover sheet.

He likes to take it to the client himself if possible, otherwise he uses FedEx.

37

"Dancing Elephant," 1983

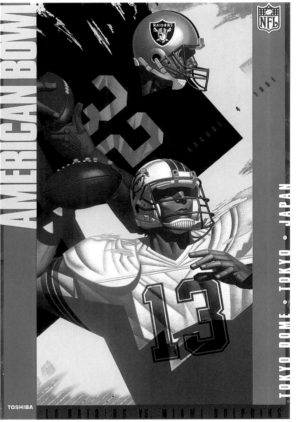

left: "Mardi Gras," 1984, right: "Football," 1991

top: "Hal's Doggies," 1985, bottom: "Hawaiian Cruise," 1992

top left: "Goldfish Tattoo," 1993
top right: "Iguana," 1987
bottom left: "P.T. Benny," 1989
bottom right: "George Washington," 1986

"Spacy," 1985

top left: "Jazz Singer," 1996, top right: "Lady with Gun," 1995, bottom left: "Mercury," 1994, bottom right: "Piano Zoo," 1996

left: "James Brown," 1993, top: "Duke Ellington," 1990, bottom: "Charlie Parker," 1989

Born in a Buddhist temple in Kyoto, ancient capital of Japan, Hiro Kimura studied art in Hawaii and California. He has received awards from the Society of Illustrators, Communciation Arts, The Humor Show sponsored by the Society of Illustrators, Illustration West, The Washington, D.C. Art Directors Club, among others. He's been featured in graphics publications such as *IDEA* magazine, where he was profiled by Seymour Chwast. His association with the Pushpin Group has led to exhibitions in Europe and Japan. Among his many corporate clients are Anheuser-Busch, Atari, Coca-Cola, Estee Lauder, First National Bank, General Electric, General Foods, Gillette, Hewlett-Packard, IBM, Intel, McDonald's, Mitsubishi Electric, the National Football League, NYNEX, Seagrams, Southwestern Bell, and Time/Warner. He has worked for many publishing clients including *The Atlantic Monthly*, *Golf Digest*, *The New York Times*, *The New Yorker*, *Newsweek*, *Time*, Berkley Books, Dell, McGraw-Hill, Random House, and Ziff-Davis.

RAFAL OLBINSKI, WHO MOVED
TO AMERICA FROM HIS NATIVE POLAND
14 YEARS AGO, LISTENS TO
OPERA WHILE HE WORKS IN
HIS BROWNSTONE STUDIO IN
NEW YORK CITY. WHEN HE
ISN'T PAINTING HE WRITES
SHORT STORIES, WHICH HE
ALSO ILLUSTRATES. HE LIKES
THE WORK OF MANY
ARTISTS, INCLUDING BALTHUS
AND BOTERO, WHOSE SENSE
OF HUMOR AND VITALITY
IMPRESS OLBINSKI. "IT'S A
GOOD THING TO LAUGH
NOW IN MODERN ART, EVERY-
THING IS SO SERIOUS."
OLBINSKI SAYS HE IS

perceived by clients as a conceptual artist, so when art directors cannot come up with ideas, they call him. Therefore, our "Time" assignment was not so unusual for him. Part of the pleasure of a job is to come up with the concept. "It is not just in the hand of the painter, but also in the brain."

Generally, a client will call him to discuss the subject matter or text of an advertisement. Then Olbinski sends sketches that are exactly the opposite of what's been discussed! Although the sketches are rough, "it's not a problem, because the client has seen my portfolio and knows what to expect in the execution of the final product. This way, they are not scared to death."

He supplies the client with six or seven sketches. Often the ideas are quite different from one another. He's found this is good for him. In the past Olbinski would come up with only one concept that he was "totally in love with ." This sometimes made it difficult to fulfill a client's needs. "It's much better to present many choices, provided I believe in all the ideas." In general, the choice is quickly made, though there is the

rare picky client and the process "drags on forever." Olbinski has found that most clients do not pick his favorite idea. At this point in his career he will try to push for his favorite concept, usually something that could serve in his gallery work as well.

He begins the assignment by referring to his own sketches from previous jobs. "Very often it creates

fresh ideas. In this case, I had been working on a series of clowns, so this job was in line with what I was doing. Clowns are a main element in my work."
He finds it very difficult to explain exactly how ideas form. "Things around you are coming to the rescue." He thought about night and day, and "the passing of time, which is a sad thing. It is our worst enemy. I thought of a nostalgic mood." At age 50 Olbinski values his time and is more selective about what he does with it. "I'm not watching stupid movies any- more; I choose the best opera, the best theater, the best food and wine. This subject matter came at the right time for me."

1 Olbinski begins by sketching a variety of concepts using a Koh-i-noor Technigraph pencil. Although he rejects the hourglass with the cloud inside for this assignment, he feels it would make a nice gallery painting. Sometimes he makes adjustments to an illustration to remove a product or create a more poetic mood so it can be exhibited in a gallery. At this point Olbinski does not need any refer- ence, he knows how a clown's ruffle looks.

2 He submits four sketches by fax for consideration. We agree that the clown is a strong visual and one that Olbinski is eager to work on.

3 The hand is the most critical element in the piece and difficult to draw. He takes Polaroids of his daughter Natalia's hand to get the proper gesture, then makes a study on whatever paper is lying around—he is not partic- ular.

4 He chooses a number of photographic references in fashion magazines to determine the angle of the clown's face and how the fabric falls on the sleeve. In one of the photos the proportions were a "perfect fit."

5 He completes the charcoal drawing on charcoal paper, though for purposes of the assignment, he says he could be using butcher paper. However, because even this draw- ing may end up in a gallery, he's become more careful about what he works on. He now sets his drawings with spray fixative for the same reason.
At this point he has refined the sketch by correcting the propor- tions and the angle of the head, delineating the shadows and the light, refining the clothing and the hand according to the reference.

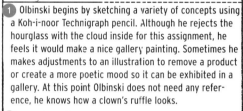

6 He traces the charcoal sketch using his mechanical pencil, which he prefers because "it's red and easy to find on the drawing table."

7 An old plate serves as a palette. He's been using this one for five years, after the one he'd had for ten years broke, "Which gave me a pain in my heart."

8 Olbinski uses acrylic paints. Though he is not particularly attached to any brand, in addition to Liquitex and Winsor and Newton paints, he prefers PÇpÇo from France and the Japanese Holbein brand for their interesting colors.
The dominant color is made by mixing White with Holbein Compose Blue #2 (similar to Cerulean Blue), and PÇpÇo Royal Blue (similar to Cobalt Blue). He works with a large #2 round bristle brush. He uses gesso, not tube acrylics, for his whites.

9 The canvas is stretched and taped to a plywood board. For larger pieces he works at an easel, for smaller ones at his drawing board. He purchases prepared canvas but gives it one more layer of gesso. Here he's laying down the background color—the blues mixed with White gesso.

10 This is the final drawing, traced in Step 6, ready to be transferred to the canvas.

11 To create a transfer, he outlines the drawing on the back of the tracing paper using a White charcoal pencil. He calls it "a very primitive method."

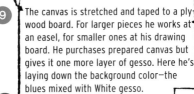

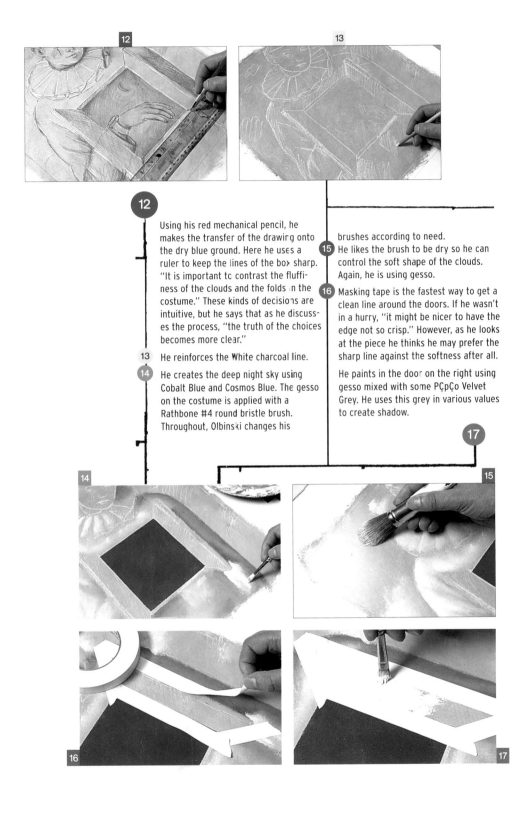

12 Using his red mechanical pencil, he makes the transfer of the drawing onto the dry blue ground. Here he uses a ruler to keep the lines of the box sharp. "It is important to contrast the fluffiness of the clouds and the folds in the costume." These kinds of decisions are intuitive, but he says that as he discusses the process, "the truth of the choices becomes more clear."

13 He reinforces the White charcoal line.

14 He creates the deep night sky using Cobalt Blue and Cosmos Blue. The gesso on the costume is applied with a Rathbone #4 round bristle brush. Throughout, Olbinski changes his brushes according to need.

15 He likes the brush to be dry so he can control the soft shape of the clouds. Again, he is using gesso.

16 Masking tape is the fastest way to get a clean line around the doors. If he wasn't in a hurry, "it might be nicer to have the edge not so crisp." However, as he looks at the piece he thinks he may prefer the sharp line against the softness after all.

He paints in the door on the right using gesso mixed with some PÇpÇo Velvet Grey. He uses this grey in various values to create shadow.

Olbinski has favorite colors for making flesh tones. The under painting is Burnt Sienna and Holbein Brilliant Yellow.

19 Over the under painting, he draws a brown charcoal line using an Othello pencil to recreate the clown's face. Then he paints over the charcoal with Burnt Umber to reinforce the line.

20 He lightens areas of the face using Holbein Brilliant Yellow and gesso. He likes the liquidity of the gesso. On the brush is Cadmium Red Light which he uses for the clown's makeup. He wants to keep the makeup delicate, not too strong. His clowns are in the European style. They are "tired clowns, their colors are faded."

21 With a White charcoal pencil he draws the hand, moon, and stars into the night sky.

22 Olbinski works as fast as possible. It only takes two hours to reach this stage of completion because he says he's learned some tricks. There was a time when the clouds could have taken two weeks. "Now I do them in ten minutes and they are much better than when it took me ten days!"
For Olbinski working from the darkest tone to the lighter tones is much faster than going from light to dark and "having to paint around each shape." Rather than drawing each cloud with a small brush, he uses a large soft one so the shapes "are coming by chance, which makes for additional excitement. You never know what will be the final result. You feel like the creator, the God, the maker of wind and clouds."

23

The hand is Yellow and Burnt Umber. The darkness in the shadows is Burnt Umber or Sepia.

24

To define the shape of the hand he lightens the area around it with Cosmos Blue mixed with Ultramarine Blue.

25

He highlights the fingertips using Brilliant Yellow and White.

26

White charcoal defines the shape of the folds of the ruffle.

27

He paints in the highlight on the fabric using gesso.

28

The shadows are a mix of PÇpÇo Steel Blue plus Cobalt Blue, and White.

29 Detailing the shadows with Steel Blue.

Because Olbinski's own watch was being repaired, he made it up. "I know what a watch looks like. Besides, the symbolism of the watch is more important than the object. The gold of the watch is also symbolic. The red band is more visible and it corresponds to the clown's cheeks." It is Cadmium Red Light mixed with Burnt Umber for the shadow.

The moon and stars are White plus a little Ultramarine Blue, though some of the stars are all White for variety of luminosity.

The lips are Cadmium Red Light with White highlights for both the nose and lips. He uses Sepia for the eye makeup. The hair is Burnt Umber and Sepia, with a little Yellow Ochre for a bit of warmth. "Brilliant Yellow plus White is also good for highlighting."

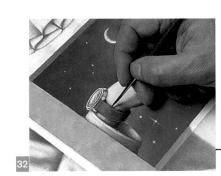

He adds Orange to the watchband to complete the painting. "It's a most fascinating pleasure. It's almost like giving birth every two or three days. It keeps you young forever. I look forward for the future; I wait for the surprises that will come with each painting. At age 20 I was stupid like a shoe. Now I know more. In painting you create your own world. A world with different rules and laws. For example, gravity doesn't apply!"

Sometimes he applies a varnish to the finished piece. He sends the rolled-up canvas to the client, or has the painting photographed and sends a transparency. He rarely makes changes and then, only small ones. His agent monitors any changes and charges for them.

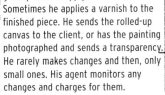

New York · Capital of the World

"New York—Capital of the World," winner of New York 95 Capital of the World contest, chaired by Mayor Rudolph W. Giuliani

top left: Illustration for *Flowers and Fables* by John Gruen, Creative Editions, division of Harcourt Brace and Company
top right: Personal work for Nahan Gallery
bottom: 25th Anniversary issue of *Smithsonian Magazine*, later used for *GEO* magazine and included in *Best of GEO* anniversary issue

114
r a f a l
o l b i n s k i

top: 31 Corporation advertising; Saatchi & Saatchi London, bottom: Assigned as a billboard for a Boston bank

Personal work for upcoming book written by the artist

rafal
olbinski

top: Personal work for the Nahan Gallery, bottom left: Annual Report for Offshore Pipelines, Inc., Pennebaker Design, bottom right: Freshfields Annual report

117
r a f a l
o l b i n s k i

top: "She Stoops to Folly" poster for South Coast Repertory Company, bottom: "The Flying Dutchman" poster for the New York City Opera

top left: Personal work for upcoming book written by the artist, top right: Personal work, bottom: Created for a Singapore bank by the Leo Burnett agency; later altered for gallery work

left: Personal work later used for a Christmas carol CD cover, right: Personal work later used for "Farewell to Narcissus" CD cover

Born in Poland and educated at the Architectural Department of Warsaw Politechnical School, Rafal Olbinski emigrated to the United States in 1982 where he soon established himself as a prominent illustrator and painter. For his work, Olbinski has received more than 100 awards including Gold Medals from the Society of Illustrators and the Art Directors Club of New York. In 1994 he won the International Oscar for the World's Most Memorable Poster, and the following year, his poster was chosen as the official "New York City Capital of the World" by a jury led by Mayor Rudolph Giuliani. His clients include *Newsweek*, *Time*, *Business Week*, *The Atlantic Monthly*, *Playboy*, *Omni*, *The New York Times*, *The New Yorker*, and countless advertising and corporate clients. His work is held in the collections of the Library of Congress Print Collection, the Carnegie Foundation, Republic New York Corporation, Equitable Capitol Corporation, Searle Corporation, Continental Corporation, Bowne & Co. Corporation, Holiday Inn International as well as numerous collections in the United States and internationally. He has been the subject of many profiles and since 1985 he has taught at the School of Visual Arts.

IT'S NOT SURPRISING
THAT FRED OTNES LIVES IN AN
IMPECCABLE, INTERNATIONAL
STYLE HOUSE OF RESTRAINED
ELEGANCE. OTNES HIMSELF IS
CALMLY SELF-POSSESSED AS HE
GOES ABOUT MAKING HIS
SOPHISTICATED COLLAGES. HIS
PREDOMINATELY GLASS HOME,
DECORATED IN WHITES, BLACKS
AND GREYS, HAS A GALLERY
WHERE THE ARTIST'S WORK
HANGS, AND A SMALL STUDIO
WITH HIS DRAWING BOARD. A
REFERENCE AREA, WITH ITS WALL
OF BOOKS AND PERIODICALS,

also has an etching press.
The large workroom/dark-
room, is where Otnes does
most of his work.
Otnes has been influenced
by or interested in many
artists and styles including
Max Ernst, Piero Della
Francesca, the Cubists ("Their
stuff doesn't move back and
forth in space"), Saul Steinberg,
Moholy-Nagy, Cy Thwombly,
Anselm Kiefer, Ben Nicholson,
Joseph Cornell, and the graphic
design of David Carson. Robert-
Rauschenberg's early work, which
Otnes first saw in Life magazine in
the 1960s, had a big impact on him.
As Otnes has developed as an artist he's found
that the means is no longer as satisfying as it was
when he began. "You can get in there and noodle a
piece to death, but that's not what interests me.
It's the art, the idea—the intellectual and visual
process that's most important."
Otnes approaches the "Time" assignment in two
ways: to cover the subject matter—which he keeps
loose because there isn't a real watch manufacturer to relate to, and for purposes of this book,
he wants to demonstrate as many technical

procedures as possible in one piece of art.
Since he began his non-painting, non-rep-
resentational collage work 30 years ago, he's
found it has certain advantages. For one thing,
he doesn't do sketches; most clients understand
that it's impossible to do sketches in collage
work. So, other than several phone conversa-
tions, Otnes is on his own.
He starts to formulate the procedure in his mind
without really nailing anything down. "In other
forms of illustration it's a bit like detective
work—you devise a plan and execute it." In
Otnes's work, the piece evolves as he works,
which he feels allows for more freedom to change
ideas. "The only thing I established was that I
wanted a surreal landscape with collage elements
related to the 'Time' theme."

1 From his extensive research files and books, Otnes assembles a variety of scrap that includes old watches, clocks, a "fascinating sundial," and other imagery relating to "Time."

2 He chooses miscellaneous elements that he feels pertain to the piece. He's really creating a "palette" of collage material. He never did find a use for the two girls on roller skates (at the left center), but he'll find a use for them some other time.

3 After selecting a number of elements from his "palette" Otnes enlarges them in his stat camera to the size appropriate to the piece. The photostat—or stat—is a negative image.

4 To make a positive of the stat, Otnes places it in his vacuum frame—a 40-IK Mercury Exposure System. The stat and 3M Color Key (a light sensitive material on acetate) are meshed by the creation of a partial vacuum. He exposes the Color Key to light. This is then developed into a posi- tive image in the darkroom. These positive "cells," combined with paper cutouts, will form the basis of the collage.

5

6

5

At this stage he keeps the composition loose and not "too predetermined." On pre-primed linen which has been mounted on plywood, Otnes begins to glue down miscellaneous collage pieces by applying Acrylic Gloss Medium. The colonnade pictured here is a print he had made on his etching press sometime in the past.

The size is "arbitrary." He makes the collage slightly larger than the finish, which will eventually be cropped to 17 1/2- by 15 5/8-inches —approximately to the scale we provided.

6 While it's still wet, he puts the Gloss Medium on the upper surface. He must move quickly to avoid wrinkling or shrinking the paper.

7 Quickly he squeegees the excess Medium from the elements with a small piece of cardboard.

8 He dries the piece with a hair dryer.

9 With a piece of cardboard, Otnes squeegees White Liquitex on the background to create a painted texture.

Between Steps 9 and 10 he affixes other collage elements onto the background, more or less arbitrarily. He looks for visuals that will make a horizon.

10 With a rag he applies a coat of Raw Umber mixed with Ivory Black oil paint (the brand is unimportant) to tone the background. Rubber gloves protect his hands.

10

7

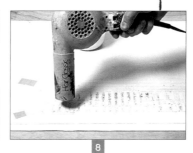

8

9

11

Otnes has rubbed off much of the oil paint, leaving a textured tone. He seals it with fixative so he need not wait days for the oil paint to dry.

12 At this point Otnes has a rough image of the total piece in his head. His primary idea is of a surreal landscape and he has created the horizon line off which the rest of the collage elements will float. Here the basic background elements are in position. They have been painted with White acrylic and rubbed with the oil paint mixture described in Step 10.
The Old Master clipping near the bottom interested Otnes because of its color and shape, as well as the fact that the head peering out of the window also created an aura of mystery. In the finish it will be obscured, though he feels "it doesn't matter if it is or isn't. It's just a dark base off which the other shapes will emerge."

13 He makes Xeroxes of various elements from those culled from his files earlier. He spray-fixes them so they won't smear, then rubs the Raw Umber and Ivory Black oil paint on with a rag.

14 With a razor blade he cuts out the elements for his "palette." This gives him a variety of options as he works.

15 To form the design, Otnes begins to move the collage elements around on the toned background: the film positives or "cells" made in Step 4 and the toned printed pieces from Step 14. This is where eye, judgement, knowledge, and experience come in.
"The opportunity of choice is so vast that it's easy to lose one's sensitivity."

15

14

13

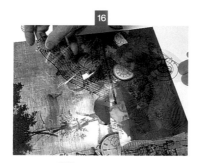

16 He moves a film "cell" to its final position.

17 Onto one piece of tracing paper Otnes traces the position of all the elements before removing them to apply the glue. He numbers each piece in the sequence in which they will go down, from first to last.

18 With the tracing as a guide, he glues the pieces down in sequence starting with the ones furthest back. With a flat brush he applies Liquitex Gloss Medium on the back of each piece, lays it down, then applies more Medium on top of the image.

19 He squeegees off the excess Gloss Medium. He repeats the gluing process until all paper elements are down on the surface.

20 The separate film cells are taped in position to a single acetate sheet, again referring to the tracing as a guide. These images, created in Steps 3 and 4, are from various sources: the tree is from an Hieronymus Bosch painting. The sundial is from a steel engraving, the lettering is from a book of old printing called *Art of the Printed Book*.

21

In the vacuum frame using Black 3M Color Key, Otnes made a negative of the arrangement of cells.

21

22 Referring to the tracing, Otnes places the negative cell in position on the artwork, tapes it on one side, and folds the cell back off the artwork. He then puts a product called 3M Transfer Key onto the surface of the artwork. This is a light-sensitive, ink-like material. Here Otnes is peeling back the piece of acetate which protects it.

22

23 He removes the acetate from the 3M Transfer Key, leaving the light-sensitive "ink" on the artwork.

23

24 With a brazer, he rolls the "ink" of the Transfer Key evenly across the surface. (Some works require five or six colors and this step must be repeated each time.)

Between Steps 24 and 25 he flops the negative cell that has been taped to one edge of the art (see Step 22) back into position over the Transfer Key artwork. He puts the art in the vacuum frame and exposes it.

25

He develops the image by pouring 3M Hand Developer directly onto the surface. This step need not be done in a darkroom, but light should not be overly bright.
He wipes the surface off with a cotton pad leaving the positive image. (Otnes points out that these images could be transferred by other means, such as silk screen. He also notes that some schools have amazing equipment for techniques such as this.)

25

24

26 With a large brush, he puts a coat of watered-down Matte Medium over the whole surface to protect it.

27 He glues down the remaining cut-out paper elements. Here he affixes the bird in the dress using the Acrylic Matte Medium.

Otnes found the dress in "a pile of rubbish"—scrap (miscellaneous images torn from magazines or books) that hadn't been filed—and liked the look of it. The bird has a surreal quality suggested by the work of Max Ernst. At first he'd tried using a human figure, but it didn't work to his satisfaction. He wanted more of a surreal feeling so he searched for the right bird head to match the body.

28 After everything is glued in position he cleans up the cut marks with a sable brush using Raw Umber and Black oil paint.

29 Here everything is in position and glued down.

Otnes used Raw Umber and Black to tone down and knock back the sky to help the smaller elements emerge. He says, "There is no logic to the whole piece." In the end he opened up the cropping because he wanted to keep more of the colonnade on the left.

"The Venetian," 1993, *Grafica* (Brazil), mixed media assemblage, 16 1/2 x 18 inches

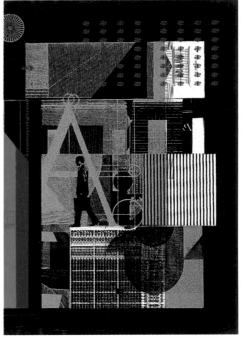

top left: The Arbi Group (Brazil), mixed media collage with photo transfer
top right: Business Brochure, mixed media collage with photo transfer
bottom left: Annual Report for Hi Tech Company, mixed media collage with photo transfer
bottom right: Interpublic Group of Companies, mixed media collage with photo transfer

top: "The Finch," 1993, mixed media collage, 21 1/2 x 24 1/2 inches
bottom: "The Day of the Fourteenth," 1992, mixed media collage and photo transfer, 21 x 24 inches

top: "The Difama," 1992, collage painting on wood mounted on canvas, 14 1/2 x 17 3/4 inches
bottom: "In the Garden," 1992, mixed media collage and photo transfer, 21 x 24 inches

top: "The Settlement, ' 1992, mixed media collage with fern, 16 1/4 x 17 1/4 inches
bottom: "On Being One Hundred," 1995 book illustration, collage and assemblage, 18 x 19 1/2 inches

133
fred
otnes

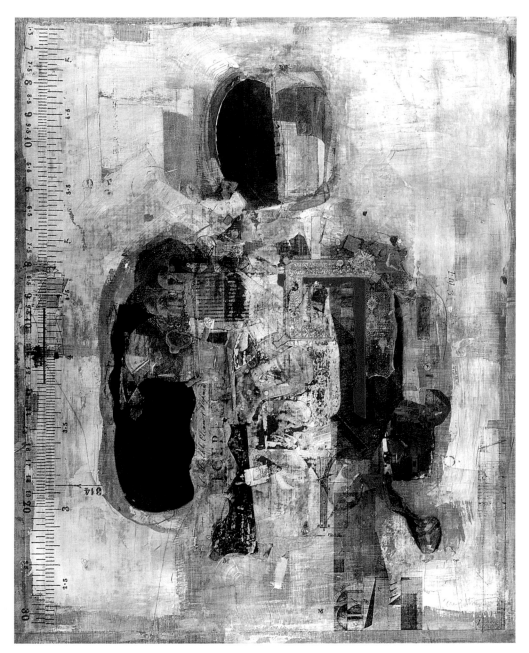

"The Acrobats," 1995, mixed media collage on linen mounted on wood, 33 3/4 x 27 1/2 inches

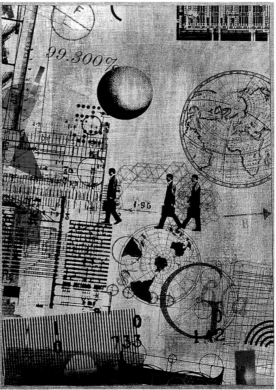

top left: Brochure Design for Hi Tech Company, mixed media collage with photo transfer
top right: The Boston Consulting Group, mixed media collage with photo transfer
bottom left: The Interpublic Group of Companies, mixed media collage with photo transfer
bottom right: Ernest & Young, mixed media collage with photo transfer

"The Gottrel," 1996, mixed media collage on linen mounted on wood, 36 x 26 inches

Born in Junction City, Kansas, Fred Otnes studied at The Art Institute of Chicago and The American Academy before moving to Connecticut in 1953. In his more than thirty years as an illustrator, Otnes's works, which combine collage, painting, and print making techniques, have earned him more than 200 awards, of which over 100 have come from the Society of Illustrators Annuals of Illustration, including their Hamilton King Award for best in show by a member. Japan's Idea Magazine cites Otnes as one of the world's best designers. His illustrations have been used for the advertising campaigns of 44 movies, for clients such as IBM, Xerox, NASA, and hundreds of other American and foreign corporations. His extensive list of editorial clients includes *The Atlantic Monthly*, *Penthouse*, *Life*, *Sports Illustrated*, and *National Geographic*. Otnes has exhibited in museums and galleries worldwide, including the Hirschorn Museum in Washington, DC; the Tokyo Central Museum; the Studio of Artists in Toyko; Umeda Museum of Contemporary Art, Osaka; Kansas City Art Institute; The Rosenwald-Wolf Gallery, University of Arts, Philadelphia; and The Reece Galleries in New York, where he has had three one-man shows.

IN THE GARAGE OF CHRIS SPOLLEN'S MODEST HOUSE IN STATEN ISLAND, NEW YORK, IS THE EVIDENCE OF ONE OF HIS PASSIONS: A VARIETY OF "HUMAN-POWERED VEHICLES" IN VARIOUS STAGES OF COMPLETION. THESE ARE BICYCLES TO THE NTH DEGREE. HE ADMITS TO BEING OBSESSIVE ABOUT THIS AVOCATION, ADDING THAT "THE ONLY WAY TO GET ANYWHERE IS TO BE OBSESSIVE. IT'S A REQUIREMENT," HE CLAIMS TO BE AN INSECURE NEUROTIC WHO DOESN'T BELIEVE IN THERAPY. "WHAT YOU GET IS WHAT YOU GET. IT'S PART OF BEING CREATIVE." BECAUSE "THE MUSE IS SO ALLUSIVE," HE'S BUILT AN ENVIRONMENT THAT'S VERY SECURE, STRUCTURED AND HAPPY. HE RELIES VERY LITTLE ON THE OUTSIDE WORLD. HE CALLS HIS MUSE A LITTLE DEVIL, AND IT IS SOMETIMES NEARLY INAUDIBLE, SO HE NEEDS A SPACE WHERE

it can be heard. "It's not really madness, it's trusting your own intuition."

Spollen has been working digitally for four years. His assistant, Noel Sibayan, "figured out the system" and they learned together. In the early days, Spollen says, "painful sparks came out of my fingers. Now, it's a wonderful way to make a living. The other day I sent an illustration of a rocket ship to the art director by modem. He transmitted his comments by e-mail. He needed another rocket ship in two hours. No problem." By the end of the day Spollen had delivered three pieces of finished art to two different locations in the city without leaving his house.

"Having done labor intensive, art driven media in the past, I'm now working in a medium that's directed to the medium that wants it. I'm doing art that's applied to the market—it's easy to download, it saves money. I'm not swimming upstream. The downside is you don't get the smells, you don't get the ink. As a result, by the end of the day you get cranky, your skin gets bad. I counterbalance it with another world, one of bikes. Going down the block at 25 miles an hour, you're sweating, alive."

When Spollen is approached for a job, the first question to him is "Do you want an inker or a thinker?" To him an "inker" means the client has the idea, the concept, and they just want a technical repetition of other work he's done. A "thinker" means the client trusts Spollen's ability to come up with a solution. After describing the general concept of the "Time" assignment, I told him to have fun with it. "When I heard that, the

hairs on the back of my neck went up," Spollen says. His initial concept was "Time is Money." The idea of day and night followed from that, and the sun and moon was a natural progression. "We'll have happy faces and rocket ships and stars...the whole thing just built itself."

THE EQUIPMENT:

Spollen's "canvas" is his monitor, a Sony 2 Trinitron 20-inch Multiscan with a Video accelerator card which tightens the images. The large monitor works in conjunction with his "palette," a 15-inch Trinitron monitor which is low level, non-accelerated. "It doesn't need that much power. It is specifically dedicated to palettes and command menus. It gives the 20-inch monitor full range and greater accuracy to the enlarged details." The mouse is the "brush" in his hands. And his cursor can cross from monitor to monitor.

His computer is a Macintosh IIci, configures to 20 RAM with a 240 hard drive. ("Which, by today's standards, is a Model A Ford"). The system has been upgraded with a 40 megahertz chip (which gives it a faster refresh rate—the time it takes to redrawn an image). It also has a video accelerator card, giving him a very sharp, refined image.

He works in Adobe Illustrator 5.5, which doesn't need the same memory as Photoshop which, he says, "eats memory for lunch." He also uses the Adobe Dimensions program. For scanning and accessing Adobe Streamline 3.0, he uses Adobe Photoshop 2.0.

His "messenger" is his Magnum Fax Modem 288. This gives him the ability to hook up with America Online which he uses as a mailbox—he puts the art work in and sends it directly to clients. Spollen also has an Internet Home Page. One of his two printers is a Hewlett Packard Laser Jet 4m, 600 DPI, black-and-white. If high-quality paper is used, it provides flawless, camera ready art. The other is a Hewlett Packard Desk Jet 1200C/Ps with an extra 12 megs of memory so it's not reliant on his computer. It can translate and print out his "heavy programs."

Why does he need a printer if he's sending disks, or clients are downloading straight from the computer? He says clients like to get a proof. Also, he doesn't trust the monitor to show accurate colors, so he uses his printer as a proofing system.

He's "so neurotic" that he has a complete duplicate system in case of crashes. For some of his two-hour deadline jobs he feels like a short-order cook, so he can't afford to wait if something happens to the system.

Every month he creates a Job File, for assignments, and a Project File. The project files are for pieces Spollen works on during professional down time, what he calls "playing." "The ability to reproduce and duplicate images you've created makes a compulsive nature more so."

1 The first thing Spollen does for every job is to input the client's phone number, address, fax number, e-mail, assignment description, etc., in his database. The folder in his file for this assignment is Society. The working title is Time is Money. Here is the printed-out file with the date the job came in. This hardcopy goes into his job file.

2 Knowing he wants a clock as the central image, Spollen sketches the clock his grandfather left him for "a little bit of reality." This three-quarter view didn't work out.

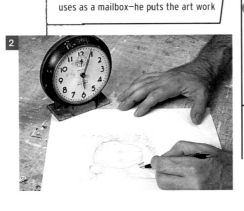

3 He plays with alternative compositions. Eventually he decides on a dollar sign in the center of the clock face because of the concept of time being money. The moon was inspired by an illustration of an evening concert series in The New York Sunday Times supplement. "I'll incorporate pieces of swipe material from a variety of sources into the art. Sometimes they can be springboards for the piece itself."

4 "I like symmetry," Spollen says, and because the elements will be so complicated, he wants a strong central image, so he decides on a frontal view of the clock. "It sounds like I know what I'm doing, but sometimes it's just a gut feeling."

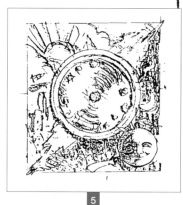

5 This is the scanned-in image of the sketch he faxed for approval. First he ran his sketch through the copier to strengthen the blacks, not only to make the fax easier to read, but for ease of scanning into his computer. It serves as the approximate rough as to where the elements will go.
He scans in the sketch, as line, at 200 DPI using a Microtek Flatbed ScanMaker 600ZS. Working in vector-based programs rather than pixel-based ones requires less memory, permitting almost all his artwork to be loaded onto 3.5 floppy discs. The discs are purchased in bulk so the unit cost is less than a subway token ($1.50); and often he does not require that the client return them.

6 Using Adobe Streamline 3.0, Spollen connects all elements of the image, making it possible to convert the entire black-and-white scan to blue, a 20% cyan. "I turn it blue like a blueprint so I can draw over it in black or dark blue and see at a glance where the scan ends and my drawing starts."
Although I only saw the rough sketch, a "real" client would like to see the "black plate" to make all compositional decisions without color. "They trust me to go to color."

7 Using the Drawing tool Spollen is ready to draw over the scanned image. After trying "every mouse in the house" he declares the Optical mouse from Mouse Systems (registered Trademark) "wonderful." It slides very easily over its metal gridded mouse pad and is very responsive. Although he was very awkward with the mouse at first, he prefers it to the stylus. "Taste and judgement dictate which tool you choose."

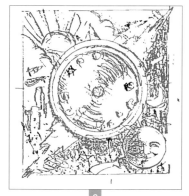

5

6

7

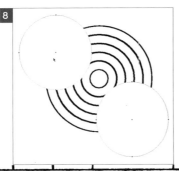

8 Spollen makes the clock in a separate window which he names exp2 (a completely arbitrary choice). He'll build each element (the sun, the moon, etc.) in separate windows.
He builds separately and together at the same time; eventually he will combine all the separate elements.
To make the clock, he first converts the Strokes to Outline and then Groups them. He creates the six concentric circles within the clock face, using the Circle in Tool Box. He makes one large circle and one small one, then, with the Blend command, selects four blends.
In Filter Box, under Objects, he selects Outline Path. The Stroke will be outlined and what was a Stroke is now a shape. At this point he groups the Strokes using the Group option. Now he can move them around as a unit, otherwise "it can become hectic if they're not grouped."
To create the final shape, he selects the Circle Tool, then hits the Shift Key, which makes perfect circles on top of the central concentric circles. Using the Merge option he combines the layers. Then by selecting each merged circle and hitting Delete, he cuts away the excess, leaving only a portion of the concentric circles.

9 To add color to the Outlined Strokes Spollen selects Red/Yellow in the Gradient box. Steel Bar Red and Yellow are pre-made gradients which reside in the Gradient Box and which are "close friends of mine." He makes decisions about the color and intensity of his gradients by eye. If he likes a color in another piece of art, he'll cut and paste it into his current job. It automatically goes into the Gradient Box.
To give the Strokes dimension he duplicates them, then selects the Black Fill command. He then selects the grouped Strokes, hits Shift/Option thereby making a duplicate set. He selects Arrange and Send to Back, which creates a drop shadow.
For the background he makes a Circle, then gives it a Black and White Gradient. The Directional option in the Tool Box determines the light and shadow placement.

10 For the clock hands Spollen selects Stroke to give it weight. In Filter, he selects Add Arrowhead in the Stylize option. "I literally asked it to add an arrowhead."
To color the clock hands or make a drop shadow, he must make the elements into one shape, which he does by using the Merge option.

11 Spollen monitor showing the Arrowhead option.

12 He "jazzes up" the image by playing with or "finessing" the gradients. The bands that were originally orange and red, he makes "more into a rainbow thing going from Grey to Orange to Pink." The Black drop shadows he changes to Grey. He's also added a White stroke along the edges of the colored bands—all this is done from the Gradient Box as in Step 9.
He uses three separate groupings to create the illusion of a highlight, a middle light, and a low light. This is done by taking the shape of the stroke, copying it

two additional times, and giving one a high color and one a low color. This gives the illusion of depth.
To create a drop shadow, he simply gives the arrowheads a Black-and-White gradient.
He makes the circles to indicate the clock numbers by selecting the Circle Icon in Tool Box and hitting the Shift Key.
The clock face is three different circles Sent to Back. One has a Red/Grey gradient, one has a Blue/Violet gradient, and one has a Light Blue gradient. Spollen gets a feeling of depth by pulling each gradient in a different direction. In reality, it's three separate circles with three gradients.
After creating the smaller circle in the lower right corner, he makes a duplicate circle and adds its color gradient. Then he selects Copperplate dollar sign in the Font option.

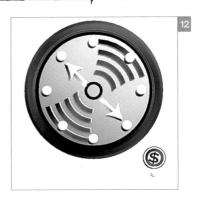

14

A view of The Moonlight Press Digital Library, Spollen's archive, which consists of 1,200 images representing 21 years of "doing it the old-fashioned way." Categories include Travel, Business, Medical, etc. Each category contains 400 images.

With his intimate knowledge of the library's contents, Spollen thinks perhaps the image of the Empire State Building would do nicely for this piece. He selects Catalogue One, selects the Business category, and scrolls through until he finds the Empire State Building. He cuts and pastes it into the artwork. In many of his jobs he adds elements he's got "sitting around digitally."

14 In the "Working Color Plate" window Spollen puts in the clock with the "blueprint" from Step 6 with some drawing in progress. This file is saved as "Working Plate," but as he goes on, he'll name the next file "Working Plate Tweeked." "I want to keep whatever state I have intact, rather than just continuing on the one—I'm afraid I'm going to lose something."

He creates the shafts of sunlight by making the shape, copying it, then sending it back. He fills one with a Red/Yellow gradient, one with White, again creating the illusion of depth by sending it back.

15 He's started to "percolate" in his "Going for More Color" window. He hasn't put the clock face in yet because it would create "too much confusion, too many layers." For dimension he adds a Black/Green gradient to the Empire State Building. He creates a sky color, a Blue gradient, and adds the sun with its Yellow/Red gradient. Here he tries a black lightning bolt with a Yellow/Red gradient highlight. He drew half of the moon's face and copied it to keep the eyes and the nose symmetrical. But at this stage, Spollen says the moon is not fully developed.

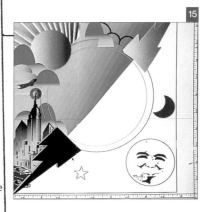

15

16 Not trusting the monitor, Spollen periodically prints out a paper proof. He says you can only really judge the colors when you see a printed proof. The colors vary up to 15% off the monitor, so after he sees a printout, he'll go back in and make adjustments. He notes that in the actual printing process, the colors from his printed proof may again vary up to 15%.

17 He decides against the black lightning which he is pointing at on the screen. He can select "100 levels of Undo in this program using Command Z." He replaces the lightning with a Red/Yellow gradient.

13

17

16

20

19

18

18 Spollen keeps a log of each job in a 3-ring binder. He uses high-quality paper for his proofs. Here he's just checking: Is that blue as good as I think it is? How about the red? "I gots to know."

19 In his "7/29/96" window he adds a Violet/Black gradient for the night area on the right. He's completed the blue sky. The clouds are gradiated ovals. When he puts one on top of the other they look like forms.
On the crescent moon he wants a bit of a glow. Using the Gradient Tool he goes from a Purple moon to a Pink moon. There are 60 gradients between the dark Purple and Pink which gave the illusion of a glow. He does the same thing with the full moon face; he gradiates from a Blue circle to a Lime circle.
Then he embellishes—making extra Pink and Red "hot" accent lines around the clock face. Under the Filter option, there is a Create option where "there just happens to be a Star option." He sprinkles stars throughout.
The airplane is from the Travel category in the Digital Library and the car is from the Auto category.
The white horizontal lines in the upper right are actually made from a "little box" option in Tool Box. This assures him that the lines are horizontal. For the lines on the middle left, he just copies the first box. "Why waste it? It also balances the composition."

20 In the "7/29/96 twk" (for "tweek") window Spollen changes his mind about the moon. After considering the brightness of the sun, the moon seems too cool. He Blends Yellow to Black which created a "delicious glow."

21 "Being politically correct," Spollen makes the sun a woman. "I did it intentionally because the moon has to be a man—Man in the Moon, right?" She's from the Digital Library. He rejected the generic sun on the "scratch pad" at the left of the screen.
He adds some rocket ships which he takes off his stationery. "I happen to have an affinity for them, and since it was my call, they're in!"
The golden balls are dimensional circles created by using Adobe Dimensions and imported into Illustrator. "In Adobe Dimensions you have two light sources giving the objects far more depth than simple gradients do, creating the illusion of a complete sphere." He then adds a drop shadow behind them.

22 He "pulls the tails" on the rocket ships and shooting stars to make them more dynamic. He uses the Hollow Arrow Tool, selects the two points that make up the tail, then hits Shift and Pull.

22

21

23 He adds a yellow circle and a red star in the middle of the night sky. "Like adding seasoning, I'm peppering the background just a little bit, getting a little more flex—making sure to balance the right-hand side because the female side was really happening."

24 Spollen had pulled proof and felt the clouds were too dark. With the image enlarged 400% he uses the Gradient Pull tool (the thin black line in the upper left), selects the clouds, and pulls the gradient to the opposite direction to lighten the sky.

25 The "Final Final 7/30/96 For output" window being prepared to be out-putted for an Iris print.
Spollen's signature is a Dorchester Script MT Font. He selects Extruded 108 horizontal, hits Fill command, and converts to Outline. (He admits that now he cuts and pastes his signature from his last job, then chooses the color based on art.)
Spollen saves the final image in an 11- by 17-inch tabloid size. He sends a disk by FedEx (or, if he's in a bind, by modem) to Manhattan Color. They can make an Iris print overnight.

26 The Iris print is on the right, Spollen's printout on the left. For reproduction he needs the Iris.

27 He ships the art to the client in a recyclable folder by Fed Ex. Although he can send art by e-mail, this is still the preferred way. In addition to the print and the disk, Spollen includes a cover letter, an invoice, and "an official gold and red stamp."
Spollen works only from 8 am to 4 pm. From start to finish this job took about a week, working on and off, though he could have done it in three days. "My eyes are like wee-wee holes in the snow by four o'clock in the afternoon. I haven't left this chair but I've lived and died a thousand times over. This work is not tactile but it's very cerebral." He says he's working more efficiently with the computer, and as he gets more proficient, he gets better and better results. He's happy.

"World Wide Web," CNP Publications

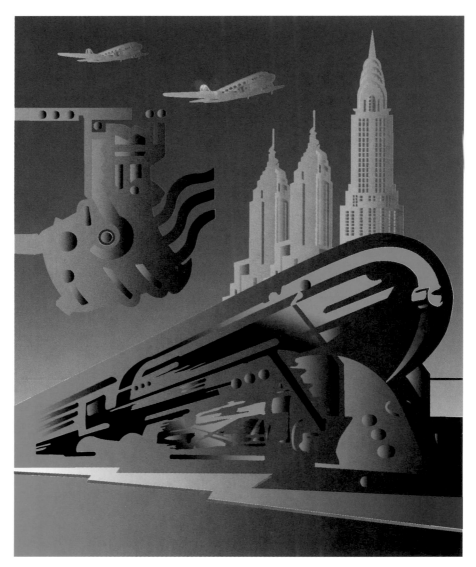

"New York Retro," Peach Pit Press

"Radio Robots," Peach Pit Press

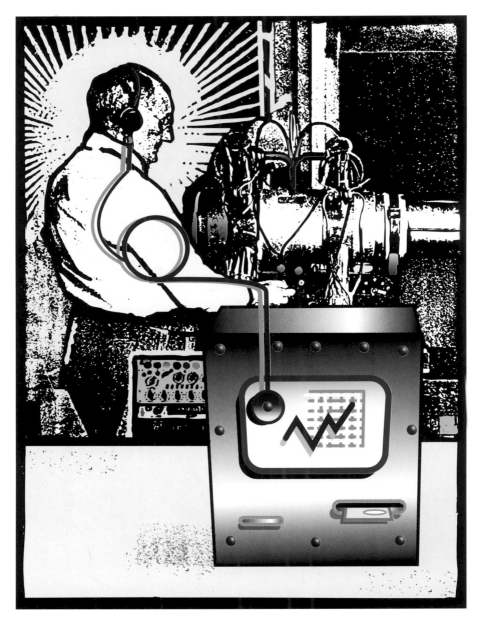

"Old Man Macintosh," Moonlight Press Studio

"Message From Cyberspace," Moonlight Press Studio

"System Crash," Peach Pit Press

"Global Transfer," Equal Net

A graduate of Parsons School of Design, Chris Spollen has used a variety of techniques to create his illustrations, including ink/template, photostat, and Xerox to produce high contrast images. The computer has been his primary tool for creating illustrations for the last four years. His Moonlight Press Studio on Staten Island has served a wide variety of clients for over 20 years, including AT&T, Citibank, Bell Labs, *Boys' Life*, *Byte Magazine*, *Consumer Reports*, *Macworld*, *PC Magazine*, *Reader's Digest*, *Woman's Day*, 20th Century Fox, HBO, Ziff Davis, and Stanley Tool Company. He has exhibited his work at the Society of Illustrators, the New York Art Directors Club, and the Staten Island Museum. He received the New Jersey Art Directors Club Award for Excellence. He has lectured at Syracuse University, Parsons School of Design, and Montclair State College.

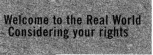
Welcome to the Real World
Considering your rights

Congratulations! You're ready to enter the professional world of illustration. Techniques sharp, you're as comfortable smudging charcoal on newsprint as you are inching a trackball across a Quark file. Your home page is up and humming, and your new portfolio is organized and professionally mounted. You're ready for your first assignment. So why doesn't the phone ring? Even more scary, what do you say when it does?

"Hello, is this Tina Newart?" a voice on the phone says. "I'm the director of the Society of Organic Asparagus Planters. We at SOAP like that Belgian endive you put on your web page. I need a pink asparagus, and I'm considering you and a number of other artists for the job."

"Cool," you're thinking, "my first real job."

"We're not-for-profit and we have no art budget," he continues, "but you'll get great exposure on the cover of our Magazine of Organic Asparagus. It reaches lots of influential people."

"Hmm," you scratch your head, "it sounds like it could be a good deal." You get hit with a shaft of brilliance. "Will I get credit?" you ask.

"Sure, sure," he says, "whenever someone calls to ask about the cover art, we'll tell them it was you." Then, as an aside, he says, "I'll fax over a purchase order. Fax it right back with your signature. It's just a formality, but our legal department insists on it."

Squinting at the faded grey type you see the words, "this work shall be considered a `work made for hire,' authorship and all rights are transferred to the commissioning agent." You call the client back and ask what this means. You discover that this organization runs the world's largest trade show on organic gardening, and they want to use your cover art as the logo. Even more, they intend selling thousands of T-shirts, aprons and tote bags with your art on them.

"Listen," he says, "there are lots of other illustrators out there who'd jump at this opportunity. Take it or leave it."

Do you take the deal? Do you walk away? Do you negotiate a compromise? Maybe you were one of the smarter ones in school who didn't cut that special class on contracts and copyright. A little more street-wise, you joined the Graphic Artists Guild as a student, and got the same benefits as the pros at half the cost. Better prepared than most of the others entering the market, you know your first client will be an executive looking for the most he can get at the lowest rate. You know he isn't a designer or an artist, he doesn't know Helvetica from Boldoni, or scratchboard from gouache—and he cares even less. Okay, so you missed the negotiation class because you were on deadline for your term project. What do you do now?

You need to organize. Join the union that represents your craft and trade—the Graphic Artists Guild. It's the best way for you to turn situations like these to your advantage. The Guild's mission is to promote and protect the economic interests of member artists. It is committed to improving conditions for all creators of graphic arts and raising the standards for the entire industry. The Guild embraces all creators of graphic arts intended for presentation as originals or reproductions at all levels of skill and expertise.

Student membership in the Guild is valid for one year beyond graduation. It's the Guild's way of helping you get on your feet. Taking advantage of Guild programs and networking opportunities will equip you with the skills you need to compete more effectively in the market, and get the best deals you can. You'll have access to the artist-to-artist hotline, the latest industry news, and the opportunity to network and learn from seasoned pros who are helpful and generous.

Every good deal you make helps not only you, but the entire industry. Every bad deal you make drags the whole industry with you. Good deals come with knowledge and experience. The Guild will give you both.

Paul Basista
Executive Director, Graphic Artists Guild

Glossary

Acrylics: Water soluble paints based on emulsion polymer acrylics thinned with water. They dry quickly, are very flexible and can be applied in thick layers. Suitable on canvas and other supports, they retain impasto and textural effects. Known for the brilliance of their color, they can imitate a variety of technical effects.

Airbrush: A technique in which pigments are applied as a controlled spray using compressed air or carbon dioxide. Subtle gradations of tone and finely blended colors can be produced by overlaying thin mists of paint. Combined with stencils or masks, they can produce hard- or soft-edged patterns.

Blending or drawing stump: Grey paper rolled to a point on one or both ends with which to rub pencil, colored pencil or pastel into gradations of tone.

Brayer: A small hand roller used to spread ink thinly and evenly over printing surfaces including plates, lithography stones, wood block, etc.

Brushes: Used for the application of paint, though also suitable for drawing with inks. Available in a large variety of shapes and sizes, they are made from different types of animal hair as well as synthetically.
    Bristle: Most important hard-hair brush, made from back of a pig, carries paint well. Range up to 12 sizes.
    Sable: Best soft hair, from the tail of the sable marten, known for strength and flexibility. Range up to 17 sizes.
    Synthetic: Inexpensive, but lack quality. Best used with acrylics which require water clean up.
    Rounds (Pointed): Round brushes that come to a point, ideal for small detail.
    Rounds (Blunt-ended) Round brushes that end in a dome shape and are used for large paint loads for wet-in-wet work.
    Brights: Rectangular shape with short hair, carry a load of paint, and can delineate sharp corners.
    Flats: Shallow, oblong brush ending in a straight edge, make angular marks, or long, broad strokes.
    Filberts: Shallow, oblong brush ending with a rounded tip offering possibilities of a flat and a round.
    Fan shaped: Used only to blend, have a thin, flat head with hair spread in a semi-circle.

Canvas: A textile support for any type of paint.
    Linen: A strong, finely woven, grey-brown cloth of medium weight available in fine and extra-fine.
    Cotton duck: Less expensive and readily available. A middleweight, soft, more open weave than linen. Both materials are available in a prepared state either stretched or in lengths with an acrylic ground not necessarily appropriate for all techniques.

Charcoal: Partially burned wood that is converted to carbon. Available in shape of original wood, as compressed charcoal, and as pencils with charcoal leads. Used primarily for sketches and preliminary drawings on painting support, though can be finished work.

Chinese ink: High quality black ink in stick form that when diluted, can produce an infinite variety of grays.

Collage: An image created by using pre-existing images or scraps of various materials glued to a support.

Colored pencils: Crayon-like leads encased in wood that can be sharpened to a fine point, made by a variety of manufacturers.

Copy shot: Reproduction quality photograph of artwork taken under color-balanced lighting for true representation of the image.

Crosshatching: Two sets of parallel strokes placed one over the other in approximately opposite directions to cover the paper or ground.

Drying oils: Vegetable oils used in painting which combine with oxygen to produce a solid film resistant to the atmosphere and many solvents.
    Linseed oil: Most durable and thorough drying of natural oils.
    Stand oil: Made from alkali-refined linseed oil, possessing improved qualities. It makes paint flow and gives an enamel-like finish without showing brushstrokes. Ages well and yellows little.

Dye marker: A large variety of markers from many manufacturers provide drawing implements in many widths and colors. They are available with water-soluble inks, permanent inks, reflective inks such as Day-Glo, and metallic inks in gold, silver and copper.

Easels: A stand on which to hold a canvas or panel while painting. Studio easels are wood and well constructed in an A shape to hold heavy works. May feature castors, screw operated raising devices to adjust level, attached paint box or brush tray. Compact table easels can be convenient for smaller areas or traveling.

Fixative: Packaged in spray cans or bottles in matte, workable, clear finishes, they stabilize the drawing surface and offer a degree of protection for pencil, charcoal, colored pencils, and pastels.

French curve: A template available in a variety of shapes including hyperboles, parabolas, and ellipses.

Frisket: Produced in sheets or rolls, frisket has a light adhesive and is used for masking areas for painting, airbrush, and stippling.

Gesso: A white, absorbent ground containing chalk or clay. Although a gesso ground can be mixed in the studio, commercial products are readily available.

Glazing: Primarily used in oil painting, glazing is the use of transparent layers of color which allow the image beneath to remain visible. When used in other media it is more correctly called a "wash."

Gouache: An opaque watercolor which can be bound with gum, though waterbased paints can be rendered opaque by the addition of white. Popular for its speed of use, its flat, contrasting colors are easily reproduced.

Ground: A base layer that acts as a buffer between the support and the painting, and gives the support a more suitable surface on which to paint.

Illustration board: A smooth-surfaced, thin board made from pasted up sheets of paper. Bristol board is a standard, quality board available in a variety of surface textures (see Paper) and thicknesses, called plys.

Liquid masking solutions: A liquid rubber which may contain a coloring ingredient to make it more visible. Good for masking large areas or highlights. Removed by rubber cement pick-up or by rolling off with fingers.

Masking: To deliberately shield an area when painting, so that when the masking is removed, the area beneath it remains untouched. Also, it can be used to protect finished areas of a painting while surrounding sections are worked upon. Low tack masking films are available for airbrush use.

Medium: An ingredient, such as oil or gum, mixed with pigment to form paint. The term also refers to mixtures added to paint in order to modify its handling properties and finish.

Oil paints: High quality pigments directly mixed with a refined drying oil, a blend of drying oils, or thickened drying oils. Prepared to a thick consistency, yet not stiff, they are rich in pigment. Commercially prepared paints in tubes vary greatly in quality. Versatile, they may be used opaquely, as glazes, or underpaintings, with or without dilution, thinly or thickly. A wide range of colors are available.

Palette: Surface for laying out and mixing paints, traditionally made from wood, though any non-absorbant surface is suitable. Ranging in size and design, most are held by a thumb hole. For acrylics, disposable paper and plastic palettes can be used. Watercolor, gouache, and tempera are generally mixed in china or plastic mixing trays with separate wells for color.

Palette knife: An implement used for mixing paint, applying thick impasto—a thickly applied paint that stands above the surface—and to scrape areas of wet oil paint to make corrections or for texture. The best are made with a forged blade diminishing in thickness for flexibility.

Pantone: The Pantone Matching System (PMS) is a system of corresponding color shades for a number of products and a variety of media. For example, colored papers, inks, and overlays will exactly match specifications for printing, if the PMS number is used to designate the color.

Paper: A sheet made of vegetable fibers matted together. Used as a support for watercolor, tempera, gouache, acrylics, pastels and drawings there are a myriad of varieties.
    Acid-free papers: Chemically neutral for long-lasting quality.
    Watercolor: Machine made with two deckle edges of consistent quality, but may lack strength and character of hand made. Rag watercolor papers sized with gelatine are highest quality.
    Weights: Expressed in pounds or grams per square meter. Lightest are 90 lbs. (190 gsm), heaviest 300 lbs. (610 gsm). Their surfaces can be hot pressed with a smooth surface with hardly any texture—which suits detailed styles of painting and flat, even applications of color—or cold pressed with a light, random grain suited to most methods of painting. Tooth, fine or smooth, describes the surface texture of board or paper.

Pastels: Pigment converted into stick form held by weak binding medium possessing a crumbly, powdery texture. Chalks are generally harder, as are crayons which are often smaller and more intensely colored. Commercial pastels may have as many as 500 shades and tints. Fixatives are used to stabilize the pastel painting surface.

Pencils: Graphite and clay bonded into a casing of cedar wood. Available in 20 degrees of hardness ranging from 9H (hardness) to 9B (blackness). HB is the middle range. Lead thickness ranges up to 1/8 inch. Best sharpened with utility knife or razor blade and repointed on fine sandpaper.

Percentage wheel or Proportion disk: A measuring device used to determine the percentages of enlargement or reduction of picture formats, similar in principle to a slide rule.

Plasticine: Commercial, oil-based modeling clay from which molds can be made.

Printmaking: A process by which an image is transferred from one surface, such as a plate or woodblock or stone, to paper (in general, though other material can be printed upon such as acetate or fabric). Some of the forms include:
    Intaglio (cutting below the surface) as in etching, engraving, aquatint, mezzotint.
    Relief (uneven surface) as in woodcut, linocut, photoengraving.
    Planograph (on the surface), as in lithograph, monotype.
    Stencil, as in silkscreen.

Projection: Optical devices to project photographic images for tracing or reference.
   Slide projectors: For 35mm slides
   Beloptican: Trade name of opaque projector for non-reflective images.

Rapidograph: The trade name for a fountain pen with a variety of nib sizes used primarily for technical drawing, but which can be used when an even line is required.

Respirator: A screen-like, filtered device worn over the mouth and nose to protect the respiratory system, used when airbrushing, or when using fixatives in unventilated areas.

Rubber cement pick-up: a rectangle of raw rubber used for swift removal and pick-up of excess dry cement.

Rub-down transfer: Sheets with adhesive backs are available in many patterns such as lines, dots, screen progressions, and letters in various typefaces which can be transferred by rubbing. Custom-made transfers can be produced by professionals or by using commercial systems available for studio use.

Scumbling: The action of dragging paint over a support, half covering it and leaving uneven, broken traces of color so the underlying paint or ground shows through.

Spray adhesive: Commercially prepared adhesives in aerosol cans for mounting artwork, type, acetate, paper and board.

Stenciling: Applying pigment through shapes cut from an impervious sheet held flush against the painting. High quality papers or heavy gauge tracing papers are acceptable, or thin plastic sheets (see Template).

Stipple: The application of a series of dots by dabbing with a brush at a right angle to the painting surface.

Support: The object upon which an image is created. There are many types beyond canvas, paper and all their varieties. Durability varies as well and must be considered when choosing supports.

Template: A guide used to render a precise shape. Standardized templates are generally made of plastic, but can be custom-made from heavy paper or vellum or cardboard.

Thinner: Materials used to thin paints for a specific consistency or for workability. Theoretically, they have a temporary effect and should evaporate during drying. They are often solvents as well. Turpentine, less expensive mineral spirits, and alcohol (which is often used for clean up), and water, are most common forms.

Transparent dyes: Available in jars and bottles, dyes stain and permeate paper and become waterproof when dry. Their brilliant colors can be utilized at full strength or in thin washes.

Underpainting: The first application of paint when utilizing a layered technique. Made in flat broad strokes, it assumes a later stage in the layering process when it will visually combine with subsequent layers to create specific effects.

Varnish: A hard, glossy oil-based substance used to coat a surface with a transparent protective layer. Paint clarity may be improved by its application as well as increased durability of the finish.

Vellum: Technically, a paper-like material made from calf-skin used as a water-based media support. The name applies to smooth, high-quality papers which resemble the real material.

Wacom tablet: Used in computer illustration, a surface upon which to draw with a stylus, which electronically transfers the line to a computer screen.

Washes: A thin, exceptionally fluid application of color made by excessively diluting paint with an appropriate thinner. Unlike glazes, no additional medium is present. Opaque colors can be applied as a wash.

Watercolor: Finely ground pigment suspended in gum arabic—a water-soluble binder. Available in tubes and pans. Fast-drying and quick to use, pure watercolor painting is based on the use of transparent washes with highlights being rendered by the white paper beneath. Generally used on paper, can be combined with other media.

Wet in wet: The action of painting into a color layer that is still wet so that the newly applied color can be worked with the existing paint.

Wet over dry: The action of painting onto a dry paint layer, so that the newly applied color does not disturb the underlying layers.

Gratitude goes to President Vincent DiFate and the Board of Directors of the Society of Illustrators for their support. Special thanks to Honorary President Howard Munce and Graphic Artists Guild Director Paul Basista for their fine words, and especially to Society of Illustrators Director Terrence Brown for his support throughout. Bravo to Marianne Barcellona for her sensitivity to the artists' work. Delight with Stephen Byram's exciting design. Thanks to copy editor Arpi Ermoyan for her endless care. Most grateful thanks to Brian Morris at Rotovision for his unwavering belief in the project, and to Angie Patchell for her cheerful help. Deepest thanks to Publications Chairman Jerry McConnell for his generous guidance. And, of course, appreciation beyond measure to the nine talented illustrators who shared their gifts so readily and with such good grace.

160